HIGH STAKES . . . MURDEROUS CHANCES

"I wanta make a play for Amon Lorrimer," Hooker said.

Gondorff looked at him and smiled. "You do, huh? You don't know nothin' about big con, and you don't know nothin' about Amon Lorrimer, but you want to make a play for him. You got a great sense of humor, kid. I'll say that for ya."

"I know he killed Luther."

"Yeah, and he's killed a lot of other people too. But their friends got brains enough to keep away from him."

"You know anybody who could do it?"

Gondorff scratched his head. "There's some guys around. Depends on if they're interested in committing suicide. An' how much we could take him for."

"Whatd'ya think?"

"Jesus," Gondorff said. "Amon Lorrimer. It'd be the con of the century, wouldn't it?"

THE STING

Paul Newman   *Robert Redford*

Robert Shaw

in a
BILL/PHILLIPS PRODUCTION
of a
GEORGE ROY HILL FILM

The Sting

A
RICHARD D. ZANUCK / DAVID BROWN
PRESENTATION

co-starring

Charles Durning	Ray Walston
Eileen Brennan	Harold Gould
John Heffernan	Dana Elcar
Jack Kehoe	Dimitra Arliss

Directed by
George Roy Hill

Written by
David S. Ward

Produced by
Tony Bill
and
Michael and Julia Phillips

A Universal Picture

Technicolor®

The Sting

Robert Weverka

Based on the Motion Picture
written by
David S. Ward

RLI: VLM 4 (VLR 4–4)
IL 8–adult

THE STING
A Bantam Book published January 1974
2nd printing ... January 1974   3rd printing ... February 1974
4th printing

All rights reserved.
Copyright © 1973, 1974 by Universal Pictures
This book may not be reproduced in whole or in part, by mimeograph or any other means, without permission.
For information address: Bantam Books, Inc.

Published simultaneously in the United States and Canada

Bantam Books are published by Bantam Books, Inc. Its trademark, consisting of the words "Bantam Books" and the portrayal of a bantam, is registered in the United States Patent Office and in other countries. Marca Registrada. Bantam Books, Inc., 666 Fifth Avenue, New York, New York 10019.

PRINTED IN THE UNITED STATES OF AMERICA

I. Chicago, 1936

1

"Hey, buddy, you got a light?"

"Beat it."

"Aw, come on, all I want is a light, for crissake."

"Don't pull that con artist crap with me, pal. I've seen you working this street for three days now."

Johnny Hooker grinned. He put down the empty suitcase he was carrying, leaned against the railing in front of a tenement house and watched the man stride away.

Zero for six, Hooker thought. Business was lousy today. He stuck the stubbed-out cigarette back into his jacket pocket and glanced up and down the street in search of another prospect.

Since eight this morning they had been working Forty-sixth and Forty-seventh Streets, and he had yet to make a score. A half block ahead he could see Luther and Kid Eirie pretending to rummage through a garbage can. He shook his head, telling them no play, and they both straightened and moved slowly on.

It was windy as hell. But Chicago was always windy as hell. Hooker picked up the suitcase and headed west again.

"Patience," Luther always told him. "A con man's biggest enemy is impatience. Slow and easy does it. And an everlastin' faith that the good Lord will provide abundantly for his chosen people." He would deliver the last statement with exaggerated solemnity. With his black face and snow white hair Luther made a perfect Bible-thumping Baptist preacher. But just as easily he could become Step 'n Fechit or a high-class fund raiser collecting funds for starving waifs in Ethiopia. He had taught Hooker everything he knew about street conning.

Up ahead, Luther and Kid Eirie rounded the corner of Clark Street, and two minutes later Hooker followed. It looked like any other street in southside Chicago—dirty. Old ladies were hanging out wash and the gutters were full of garbage.

Hooker scanned the street, sidewalks and doorways, then slackened his pace a little as he caught sight of the Italian kid a hundred feet ahead. He was standing on the steps of a tenement building lighting a cigarette. Too young to be carrying more than five or six bucks, Hooker decided. Still, his suit was new. And his slicked down hair looked like he really thought he was something. He was twenty or twenty-one, about the same age as Hooker.

Shit, Hooker thought, it was better than nothing. And maybe they would get lucky—maybe it was pay day for the guy. Hooker drew out the old cigarette butt and quickened his pace as the kid bounced down the steps and headed east.

"Hey, buddy, you got a light?"

"No."

"Aw, come on, all I'm askin' for is a light, for crissake."

"Get lost."

The kid had new alligator shoes and a jazzy manicure. Hooker grabbed his arm, smiling broadly. "Hey, come on, pal, if you can't afford a match how 'bout a light off your butt, huh?"

The kid's face was turning red, but he had stopped. He dug in his pocket and came up with a fancy lighter.

"Thanks," Hooker said. "Nice day, huh?" He cupped his hands and finally got the butt going. "Hey!" he said, suddenly looking up the street, "What the hell's going on?"

Luther and Kid Eirie had gone into action. Eirie was barreling toward them at full speed with a wallet in his hand and Luther was limping along behind, screaming bloody murder.

The Italian gave an amused laugh. "The guy must'a lifted the nigger's wallet."

"Hey, look out!" Hooker shouted. Eirie was coming directly at them. Hooker quickly pushed the Italian to the side and stuck out a foot.

"Shit!" Eirie cried. The foot caught him perfectly and he landed squarely on his chin. Hooker grabbed the wallet from his hand and backed away.

"Now get the hell out of here," he said.

"You son-of-a-bitch! You fuckin' nigger-lover. I'm gonna get you for this!" Eirie glanced at Luther and took off, barreling for the corner again.

"What the hell's the matter with you?" Luther was screaming. "You stupid peckerwood, he stole my wallet! What the hell you let him go for?"

The Italian kid's eyes were like saucers. People didn't stop pickpockets in this neighborhood—especially for niggers.

Hooker gave Luther an angry glare and threw the wallet on the pavement. "There's your fuckin' wallet, Sambo."

Luther gaped at him. He picked up the wallet and a look of great relief came to his face as he checked the contents. "Hey, man, I'se sorry. I didn't mean what I said. I'se just kinda worked up, you know. Hey, lemme give you guys somethin', huh? Is a hundred enough?"

"Naw, forget it. It was nothin'. Just get yourself to a bank with that money." Hooker picked up his suitcase.

The Italian was frowning now, looking from one to the other.

"Hey, wait," Luther said. "I got a favor to ask you guys. Please?"

Hooker scowled at him. "You can't expect much from a stupid peckerwood."

"I'll pay for it. Look, I'll give you guys five hundred bucks apiece. For you and your friend here. All you gotta do is run a little errand for me." He held out two five hundred-dollar bills, looking anxiously from Hooker to the Italian.

"Why don't you go sit on a fire hydrant and spin for a while?" Hooker sneered. "You got your money, now what the hell else do ya want?"

"Hey, wait a minute," the Italian said. "Just take it easy, huh? Let's hear what the guy has to say."

The hook was in. Hooker sighed heavily and glared at Luther. "All right, old man. You got two minutes."

A look of relief spread over Luther's face again. He glanced cautiously up and down the street. "You see, I don' know my way aroun' Chicago yet, an' I needs some help. An' you two seem to be honest guys."

"You've wasted twenty seconds," Hooker muttered.

"Will you listen to him, for crissake!" the Italian said.

Luther smiled appreciatively and turned to direct his story to the Italian. "What I'd like you to do is deliver some money for me. I need somebody I can trust."

"Why don't you do it yourself?" Hooker said.

"Will you shut your fuckin' mouth!" the Italian hissed.

"The reason I can't do it myself is the people I owe it to might try to kill me. You see, I run some slots for them down in Atlanta. They think I been holdin' out on 'em."

The Italian nodded and glanced at Hooker. Hooker sighed impatiently.

"All you gotta do is drop it in a box. They won't do nothin' to *you*. They won't even know it happened."

Hooker shook his head. "Look, I don't like to see anybody get killed. I got a train to catch."

Luther turned anxiously to the Italian. "How 'bout you? I'll give you the whole grand."

The Italian was sweating a little now. But the hook was in too deep for him to let go. "I get paid in advance?"

"In advance," Luther said. He handed over the money.

"Hey," Hooker said. "What makes you think you can trust him? He didn't do shit when the pickpocket came by."

"Why don't you butt out and go catch your train? I woulda give him the wallet if I'd got it." The Italian smiled at Luther. "Don't worry, old timer, you can trust me. Where do you want it dropped?"

Luther glanced nervously up the street again, then pulled out a sealed envelope. "Eighteen-eleven Mason Street. Just put it in box three-C. You won't have no trouble. And be careful. There's five thousand dollars in there."

The Italian slipped the envelope inside his jacket. "You got nothin' to worry about."

Hooker shook his head. "I'll tell you something, kid. You ain't gonna walk half a block with that envelope bulgin' in your pocket like that. The way you guys been flashin' money around, every pickpocket in the district knows a wad is comin' through by now."

Luther looked alarmed. "What can we do?"

"You got a bag or a handkerchief, or something?"

"I got a handkerchief," Luther said quickly.

"Okay," Hooker said. "C'mon back here." He took

them into a narrow recess between the two buildings. "Now let me have the envelope."

The Italian glanced hesitantly at Luther.

"Come on, fancy pants," Hooker said. "If you don't get with it you ain't gonna have nothin' left to put in that box but your undies."

Luther nodded and the kid handed over the envelope. He spread the handkerchief over his hand and put the envelope on top of it. "Now, you better stick your own stuff in here too if you wanta keep it."

The kid hesitated again. Then he brought out the two five hundred bills and placed them on the envelope. He searched his coat pockets and added another envelope and then his wallet to the stack.

"Now hold this for me," Hooker said. The Italian put his hand under the bundle and Hooker tied the four corners together. Hooker took the tied bundle and shoved it under his own coat and up under his armpit. "Now, carry it up here, under your armpit, like this. They can't reach it up there, right?"

It was the "switch." When Hooker drew his hand out it contained a wad of toilet paper tied in a similar handkerchief. He quickly shoved it inside the Italian's coat and under the armpit. "You can feel it all the time while it's up there. Right? Now, just leave it there. Don't touch it until you're ready to make the drop."

The Italian looked at the lump under his arm and pulled his coat a little tighter. "Yeah," he said.

"There's a cab stand about a block and a half up the street there," Hooker said. "You'd better get up there as fast as you can."

The Italian was smiling now. "Yeah. And thanks. Thanks a lot. And don't worry, old man, your drop is as good as made."

Hooker and Luther watched as the kid strode rapidly up the street. About a block away Samuelson was coming in the opposite direction, staggering a little, his fingers working nervously as if he was a pickpocket preparing to dip into someone's pocket. The kid spotted him. He made a sharp turn, angling toward the other side of the street, and then broke into a run. Hooker and Luther grinned.

When the Italian finally disappeared around a corner, they lit out in the opposite direction, laughing out loud now. Even at fifty-eight Luther Coleman was the faster runner. His limp had now magically disappeared and he'd turned into a gray-haired Jesse Owens. Halfway down the block Hooker slackened his pace a little. He jammed the empty suitcase into a trash can, then raced after the old Negro.

When they rounded the corner and headed down Clayton they flashed past Eirie, who was leaning against a wall dabbing a handkerchief to his bruised chin. As quickly as they passed, Eirie detached himself from the wall and loped after them.

At the next corner they turned again, and finallly ducked into a narrow dead-end alley. They sat down under a rusty fire escape and for several minutes said nothing, all of them trying to catch their breath.

Hooker finally shook his head and laughed. "For a minute there I thought we'd lost him. When I said he didn't do nothin' to stop the pickpocket I thought he was gonna hit me in the teeth."

"Yeah," Luther laughed. "Where's Samuelson?" Playing the drunk with itchy fingers, Samuelson was added insurance for the con, scaring the mark, keeping him moving so he would have no chance to examine the package under his arm.

"He's coming," Eirie said and laughed. "He's probably working his way back."

Hooker brought the handkerchief-wrapped bundle out from under his arm and set it in his lap. "Well, whatd'ya think?" he said, pulling at the knots.

Luther chuckled. "Ten bucks, tops."

"We shoulda taken his shoes," Eirie said. "You see the duds he was wearing?"

Hooker handed the counterfeit five hundred-dollar

bills back to Luther and picked up the wallet. It was cheap imitation leather, obviously new. He spread the bill compartment and smiled. There was a five and a one. "Six," he said.

Luther and Eirie glanced indifferently at the money. It was less than average, but better than nothing. Hooker tossed the bills to Luther and idly searched through the rest of the wallet. "Joseph Mottola," he read from an identification card. He smiled and pulled a small photograph from one of the pockets. "There you go, Eirie," he said tossing it over. "A picture of Myrna Loy."

"Hey, that's great," Eirie said dully. He picked up the picture and gazed critically at it. "Shit, it doesn't even show her tits."

Hooker leaned forward suddenly and gave a shrill whistle. Samuelson spotted them and came smiling into the alley. "How much?" he asked.

"Six. Did you see which way he went?"

"Yeah. He headed north. Full speed."

They always did, Hooker thought with a smile. Some day a mark would destroy his faith in human nature by honestly dropping the package off in the Mason Street box. "Well," he laughed, "he's got enough toilet paper to blow his nose all the way to Evanston."

"What's in the envelope?" Luther asked.

Both Luther and Hooker had been surprised when the kid put the second envelope in the handkerchief. But people did strange things. Once a man put in a tin of condoms and a half pint of whiskey. The kid's envelope might be anything from an insurance policy to love letters.

It was a large manila envelope, folded down to letter size. Hooker unfolded it and reached inside. There were bundles with rubber bands around them. He pulled them out.

They all stared, incredulous for a minute.

"Jesus Christ," Eirie said. He stuffed his bloody

handkerchief in a rear pocket and leaned forward. It was money, bundles of hundred-dollar bills.

Luther reached for a bundle. "Lemme see that."

"You think it's legit?" Hooker asked. It was hard to believe a twenty-year-old kid would have this kind of dough.

Luther pulled one of the bills out from under the rubber band and squinted closely at it. He turned it over, examined the back and then snapped the paper between his fingers. He shook his head. "Man," he said, "this is the real thing. He held it up to the light.

"How much?" Samuelson asked.

Hooker counted the bundles. There were five, each with twenty hundreds, and another with ten. He whistled softly. "Eleven grand."

Luther took another bundle and spun slowly through it.

"God damn!" Samuelson breathed.

They were all grinning now, except Luther. "Whatd'ya think?" Hooker said.

Luther looked worried. "I don't know. What was that guy's name?"

Hooker picked up the wallet. "Joseph Mottola."

"You guys ever hear of him?"

None of them had.

"He could have won it," Hooker said. "The ponies or the numbers."

"Yeah," Luther said doubtfully. "It's possible."

Hooker knew what the old Negro was thinking—that the Italian kid might have been a runner for a bookie joint or a numbers spot. Lifting that kind of money was suicide.

"Aw, come on, Luther," Hooker grinned. "Every time we score more than a hundred bucks you get nervous. Maybe the kid hit it lucky on a number. He had a new suit. Maybe he was just a messenger boy for a big plunger. A guy maybe hit a big winner and he sent the kid to pick up the dough."

"Yeah," Luther shrugged. "Maybe so."

As the veteran of the group, Luther generally kept half the take. Today he took only two of the bundles. He tossed Hooker three thousand, and Samuelson and Eirie four thousand to split. He pulled himself to his feet. "We'd better get outa here. You gonna be down at Boudreau's tonight?" he asked Hooker.

"Yeah."

"Okay, I'll meet ya there at ten. Somethin' I wanna talk to ya about. And try to hold onto some of that dough, huh?"

Hooker nodded and watched the old Negro shuffle off toward the street, then he spun through the bundles of money. Jesus, three grand!

2

Meyer saw him coming. Through the dust-clouded window he saw Johnny Hooker striding across the street toward his pawn shop. And from the way Hooker was walking, he must have found himself some money. He would be coming in to get the suit and the radio he had pawned two months ago. Meyer liked Johnny, but he didn't smile. The woes of the world were too heavy on his stooped shoulders to permit it. He lowered his chin and peered over his small, steel-rimmed glasses, as Hooker came bursting through the door.

"How are you, Mr. Meyer?" Hooker grinned, looking happily around at the dusty array of junk.

Meyer gave an imperceptible shrug. "Your suit is back there. The radio's on the shelf."

Hooker pulled out his wallet. "How much I owe you?"

"Three dollars, plus a dollar-eighty. Four-eighty."

Hooker tossed a five on the counter. "Keep the change."

Meyer pulled open the shallow drawer under the counter and dropped the five into it. He sighed and shook his head. "'Keep the change,' he says. So now I'm a shoeshine boy living on tips." He brought out two dimes and placed them neatly on the glass counter. But Hooker was already searching through the rack for his suit. He found it—a dark blue double-breasted with pinstripes—and moved to the shelf of clocks and radios. "You're a good man, Mr. Meyer," he said over his shoulder.

Meyer nodded. "I'm a good man, you're a good man, we're all good men. So why is the world so bad?"

Hooker laughed. With the radio under one arm, he shook the suit, liberating half a pound of dust. "Hey, this suit is dirty."

Meyer grunted. "Cleaning I don't do. You want cleaning, take it to Bauer down the street. Bauer don't loan money, I don't do cleaning."

Hooker stared at him for a moment, then grinned. "That makes sense," he said, and turned for the door.

Meyer watched the kid struggle to get the door open and squeeze his way out, the big grin still on his face.

Johnny Hooker was a smart kid. A very smart kid. Sooner or later the other punks his age got in a little trouble. But Johnny was smart. Johnny would get in *big* trouble someday. Really big trouble.

Meyer picked up the two dimes and lifted his head to look at them through his glasses. Forty-six years. He had been in the pawn business forty-six years now, and this was the first tip he ever got. So maybe prosperity was just around the corner.

"Is it any good?" Hooker asked.

"You think I make a living selling champagne that isn't any good? You think that's why all my customers come back? To buy no-good champagne?"

The magnum of champagne stood in the window of

Neuman's Delicatessen surrounded by dusty cheeses, salamis, and canned oysters.

"Well"—Hooker shrugged—"you know. I thought it might be just for display or something."

"Look at the label," Mr. Neuman reached impatiently over the little curtain and tapped the bottle with his greasy butcher knife. "Genuine champagne. 1932." He glanced back at the counter, where two customers were waiting. "So you want it or not?"

"Can you ice it for me?"

Mr. Neuman gave him an exasperated look. "Sure, sure, and I could put it in a gold-plated ice bucket. You think this is the Waldorf?" He sighed impatiently and headed back into the store, wiping the knife on his apron. "Come back in three hours," he muttered. "I'll have it iced."

When he got back to his room, Hooker borrowed a whisk broom from the landlady and cleaned up his suit. He took his wallet with him when he went down the hall to the bathroom. He shaved, took a bath and returned to his room to dress. His shirt was a little yellow around the collar, but nobody would notice that.

After three attempts, he got his necktie straight. He returned the whisk broom to Mrs. Lydecker, and went out the front, whistling as he headed west.

The wind had died down. It was almost dark now. Men with lunch pails were hurrying home, and the cars were switching on their lights as they whined along the crowded streets.

Hooker walked down to Angie's Diner at the waterfront, where he had a couple of pork chops and mashed potatoes, along with two pieces of apple pie. People didn't generally wear suits and ties into Angie's, and Hooker was appropriately noticed.

"Looks like it's gonna be a nice funeral, Hooker. What time you bein' buried."

Even Angie leaned out from his kitchen and shook his head. "Better put a bib on him tonight, June."

Hooker pretended not to hear.

"Got a big date?" June, the waitress, asked when she delivered his pie.

"That depends." Hooker smiled. "What time you get off?"

She laughed and hurried off, moving frantically to keep up with the evening rush. She was a cute little blonde with broad hips and an amazingly narrow waist. Someday he would ask her seriously, Hooker told himself. He left a five under his plate.

Hooker picked up the chilled champagne at Neuman's. He bought a stack of records in a music store and headed for Maggie Carr's Emporium on Forty-second Street. Maggie's was a cheap whorehouse occupying the second floor of an old office building. She had worked con with Luther before going into business for herself. She was in her fifties and plump now, but as full of beans and as thickly covered with rouge as always. She greeted him with hugs and took him into the parlor, where he was immediately surrounded by a dozen half-dressed girls who proceeded to play his records and drink his champagne.

Maggie's business hours were between nine at night and four in the morning, and there were no regular customers around. Maggie recommended a new girl from New Orleans named Louise. Hooker spent a half-hour with Louise, and then another hour with the other girls who came giggling through the door demanding to join the fun.

When the first of the paying customers began to arrive, Maggie hustled the girls off to work and sat on the bed while Hooker dressed.

"How's Luther gettin' along?" she asked.

"Great. He told me to say hello."

"Bull crap. Tell him to come around sometime and say hello himself. Old Luther's a hell of a guy, isn't he?"

"Aw," Hooker said, "he's just a dumb old nigger.

Niggers don't know nothin'." He splashed water in his face and waited for the explosion.

He could hear the long intake of breath. "Johnny Hooker," she said tightly, "you're the most ungrateful bastard I have ever met in my entire life. After all that man has done for you? If it weren't for Luther, you'd still be a stinking panhandler."

Hooker turned and grinned at her. She stared at the impish smile for a moment and then huffed indignantly, her mascaraed eyes narrowing. "Johnny Hooker, you're a shit."

"And you, Maggie, are the most beautiful girl in the whole world." He kissed her on the forehead and tucked a hundred-dollar bill into her bra.

She pulled out the bill and threw it at him. "I don't want your goddamned money."

Hooker picked it up. "You peddlin' your girls for nothin' nowadays?"

She waved the money away, but she couldn't play mad anymore. "Aw, c'mon." She laughed. "You brought records and champagne, and the girls had a lot of fun. It's good for 'em once in a while."

"I'll tell you what I'll do," Hooker said. "I'll invest it for you over at Moffitt's. I'll bring you back five hundred." Moffitt's was a gambling joint on Forty-fourth, a fast basement operation run by one of the North Side syndicates. Over the years they had taken several hundred bucks from Hooker. But his luck had been running bad too long for that to continue.

"Hah!" Maggie snorted. "I'd like to see anyone walk out of Moffitt's with five hundred dollars. If you're smart, you'll stick it all in your mattress."

"You kidding? This is my lucky day, Maggie. A lady just threw a hundred-dollar bill at me."

"Yeah."

Moffitt's had been a soup kitchen when Hooker had first come to Chicago five years ago. Then it had been a storehouse for repossessed cars before Moffitt turned it into a gambling joint. It had looked better when it was a soup kitchen.

Eddit Moffitt was sitting on a high stool overlooking the four crowded crap tables at the front of the room. Hooker waved to him as he made his way toward the roulette wheel, and Moffitt responded with an almost imperceptible nod. Except for the cigar in his hand, Moffitt always looked like he was asleep on that stool. But under the half-closed lids his eyes were constantly shifting, watching the bets and the dice and the quick hands of the croupiers. According to Luther, he had once been a trigger man for Al Capone.

Three people were sitting at the roulette wheel, with Jimmy Caine, an ex-pickpocket, standing behind the table handling the bets.

"Hey!" Jimmy smiled and stuck out a hand. "Look who's here. How you been, Hooker?"

"Fine. How's the roulette business, Jimmy?"

"Not bad. Beats workin' the alleys. Okay, folks," he said to the bettors, "place your bets. Round and round she goes." He gave the wheel a slow spin and started the ball in the opposite direction. "How's old Luther gettin' along? He teachin' you anything?"

"Yeah. He said to say hello."

Jimmy laughed. "Yeah, I'll bet he did." Luther's attitude toward gambling was well known. "Shit," he'd drawl, shaking his head with disgust, "it's like flushin' your money down a toilet and hopin' some of it will float back up."

Hooker laughed and pulled out his wallet.

"You gonna have a go?" Jimmy asked.

"Maybe. What's good tonight?"

"They're all good." Jimmy laughed. "Some are good for you, some are good for the house. The four to nine's been hot tonight. Or why don't you try a ten spot on twenty-eighth street down there. Pay ya ten to one."

Hooker nodded and looked over the board. The other players were distributing dollar bills and coins over the numbers. The chance of any single number coming up was thirty-eight to one against the bettor. And then there were all kinds of combinations paying lesser odds. He could spread his money around. Or he could do it fast—put everything on red or black, which paid even money. Hooker slid the bills from his wallet and tossed them all down.

"Four grand on the black."

Jimmy had spun the wheel, but he held the ball and stared at Hooker. The two men and the woman were gaping at him.

"You sure you wanna start off that big?" Jimmy asked. "A bet like that could really dent us, Hooker."

He had tossed the money down on an impulse. But for some reason he felt confident. "I feel lucky tonight." He smiled.

"Aw, come on, Hooker, why don't you just—"

"Three grand on the black, Jimmy."

Jimmy sighed. He glanced toward the big man on the stool at the front of the room and sent the steel ball whirling around.

While the ball was spinning, the woman looked quickly at Hooker. She smiled and layed a five-dollar bill next to his stack of hundreds. Unnoticed by anyone, Jimmy's foot moved to a concealed lever beneath the table. The lever controlled a series of hidden magnets within the wheel, for the express purpose of making sure the ball didn't hit any undesirable numbers. Jimmy hated to do this to a friend, but at fifty-eight he couldn't afford to be unemployed—or dead.

Hooker watched the little ball slow down and drop toward the numbers on the wheel. It bounced several times, skipping up toward the center, and then as Jimmy's foot hit the lever, it seemed to jump sideways and stop abruptly.

"Twenty-seven," Jimmy said grimly. "Red."

Hooker felt a slight jolt inside his stomach. He had been almost certain it was going to fall in black. He gazed woodenly at it and slowly nodded.

"Sorry, Hooker," Jimmy said as he gathered in the losing bets. "But maybe it's a good thing. A guy could get in trouble around here losin' that kind of bet." He glanced pointedly toward the front of the room again.

Hooker looked at him, then followed the glance. Eddie Moffitt had shifted on his stool. He was facing the roulette table now, still motionless, the half-closed eyes impassive, but their message clear. Hooker turned back, and Jimmy gave him a half-shrug.

"Spin it again, Jimmy," Hooker said.

"Now, wait a minute, Hooker."

"Just for the fun of it."

Jimmy spun the wheel and gave the ball a spin. This time the ball made no sideways jumps. It bounced a couple of times and settled into number fourteen, black.

Jimmy looked up, a sick look on his face.

"Don't worry about it." Hooker smiled. "I knew it was my night."

3

Once he got out of the heavy traffic, Arthur Greer pushed the Ford up to sixty and headed north along the waterfront. He was carrying bad news, information that he knew would bother Coombs. And it would bring an angrier reaction from the top level in New York. And yet Greer felt a secret pleasure in his mission. He had done his job perfectly. He had contacted a dozen people. He had successfully traced down the leads and reconstructed exactly what had happened. The fact that Mr. Coombs's worst suspicions had been verified was not his fault. Some people would be in big trouble after today. They would be moving down in the organization. But twenty-two-year-old Arthur Greer had once again shown that he was dependable, a young man on his way up. He whipped the car through the gates of the Lakeview Cannery and sent a cloud of gravel flying as he skidded to a halt at the front door.

He jumped out of the car and walked rapidly past the dimly lit front offices and back to the service elevator. At the third floor he threaded his way through the darkened warehouse area and finally into the counting room.

The room was large, the desks and tables illuminated by a dozen florescent lights hanging from the high ceiling. It was more or less a clearinghouse, a makeshift office in which all the transactions for the city's numbers games were handled. The betting slips and cash from the outlying spots were delivered by six o'clock. By nine or ten the slips were collated, and the number receiving the lowest play in the city was then declared the winner for the day.

The tabulating and counting had already been completed when Greer strode into the room. The accountants and bookkeepers were covering their adding machines and packing up for the day. They gave him only indifferent glances as he skirted around their desks and disappeared into Coombs's corner office.

Al Coombs was a quiet, balding man with eighty pounds of excess flesh at his midsection. After forty years in the rackets there was very little that could surprise him. He looked up dully as Greer burst into his office. He already knew what the kid was going to say.

"We found Mottola," the boy said. "It was rough, but I traced him down."

Coombs nodded. Arthur Greer would say it was rough if he was sent to the drugstore for a pack of cigarettes.

"He was drunk in a dive over on Lombard. Bartender said he'd been there all day."

Coombs looked thoughtfully around his desk. "I don't suppose he had the money."

"He lost it to a couple of con artists on his way out of the spot."

"How much?"

"Eleven thousand."

It was more than Coombs expected, too much for Keyes to have trusted with a new kid. "Who were they?"

"I don't know yet. Mooney's checking it out. But one of them was a nigger.

Coombs sighed wearily and squeaked forward in the chair. "All right. You'd better get on the phone to New York. See what Lorrimer wants to do about it." He snorted softly. "I got a pretty good idea, though."

Amon Lorrimer was not at home. The call from Chicago was transferred from his Long Island estate to the Regency Club in Manhattan, where Mr. Lorrimer was expected to be until midnight.

Joseph Leonard, one of Lorrimer's assistants, listened to Arthur Greer in stony-faced silence. He grunted several times, said, "I'll let you know," and hung up. He moved quickly out to the gambling room where Lorrimer was shooting dice. He stopped several feet away from the table, then stood patiently waiting for the opportune moment to approach. Mr. Lorrimer did not like to be interrupted when he had bets riding.

Lorrimer was in his early fifties. He was short and stocky, with a feathering of gray at the edges of his neatly brushed black hair. He wore the same fashionably cut tuxedo as the other gamblers, and his nails were perfectly manicured. But there was still a touch of coarseness about him. In contrast to the soft elegance of the surroundings and the casual air of the other patrons, Lorrimer had the hard look of a man who had fought his way to the top, and had not been hampered by scruples on the way.

"Seven away, line loses," the croupier finally droned. Joe Leonard moved up.

"Amon, can I see you a minute?"

Lorrimer gave him an impatient look. He had already started distributing bets over the table.

"It's important," Leonard said.

Lorrimer made a slight finger motion, indicating to the croupier that his bets were off, and moved away from the table.

"What's the matter?"

Leonard glanced around and kept his voice low. "We had a little trouble in Chicago today. One of the runners got hit for eleven grand."

Lorrimer's mouth twitched, but his eyes were solid. "Which one?"

"A kid named Mottola."

"They sure he didn't pocket it?"

"No, they checked his story with a tipster. He was cleaned by two grifters on Forty-seventh. I can get their names for you."

"I don't care about their names. Were they working for anybody?"

"I don't know. We're running that down now."

"Okay. Get somebody local to take care of it. And do it fast. We gotta discourage this sort of thing."

Leonard nodded and turned away.

"One more thing," Lorrimer said, stopping him. "While you're at it, buy that Mottola a new pair of shoes."

"Right."

Hooker had no particular regrets about losing the money. He'd had more fun than if he'd stuck it in his mattress.

That kind of living didn't make much sense to Hooker. And maybe next time he tossed a wad on the table things would come out better. It all evened out.

Hooker knew Luther would chew his ass when he heard about it. Luther was the only guy in the world

he'd take any heat from. Not even his old man.
George R. Hooker was a horse's ass who never had a
dime except for bootleg booze, and the last time
Hooker saw him he was standing by a fence with a
belt in his hand. Hooker was fourteen then, and since
he'd hopped that freight for Chicago he'd heard nothing
more about Rockford, Illinois, or George R.
Hooker. He had no regrets about that, either.

The funny thing was, Luther Coleman had chewed
him out the first day they ever met. The old Negro
was conning a guy on the corner of Forty-third Street,
and Hooker had wandered up to see what was going
on, and he'd queered the whole play. The mark walked
off, and Luther stood there for five minutes telling
Hooker what a stupid son-of-a-bitch he was. Hooker
never did figure out why he took it. That had been
three years ago, and Hooker had been working with
him ever since.

What amazed Hooker about Luther was the old
man's versatility. One minute he could be a shuffling,
sad old Negro who couldn't speak a word of understandable
English, and the next minute he could talk
like a college professor. Hooker had never met anyone
quite like him.

Boudreau's was in the basement of an old tenement—a
boiler room that had been converted into a
bar. There hadn't been a whole lot of converting. The
pipes and heater vents still hung from the ceiling and
cracked a head now and then. But at least it was
warm.

It was also crowded and noisy. Hooker spotted Luther
and Eirie at a table in the far corner, and carried
a beer over from the bar.

"You're late," Luther said. "Where ya been?"

"I had a couple of appointments."

"Moffitt's?"

"Yeah."

"How much ya lose?"

"All of it." It sounded worse now, telling it to Luther. The old Negro just stared at him. He finally sighed and shook his head.

"You're a stupid son-of-a-bitch," he said. "You coulda been nailed, sprayin' money around like that."

"Naw," Hooker said quickly. "I checked the place out. There weren't no dicks around." The statement was half-true. He had looked around at the other gamblers, but he hadn't thought much about cops.

"You're a con man," Luther said, "an' ya blow your money like a pimp. I didn't teach ya to be no pimp."

Hooker had no answer for that. But it was over, he decided. Luther had gotten it off his chest. The old man looked off at the crowd again, and Eirie gazed sleepily at the table. Hooker lifted his beer bottle and let half of it slide down his throat. Behind him, people were laughing, telling each other about their day's business, planning new cons for tomorrow. Most of Boudreau's customers were street people—grifters, con artists, and part-time burglars. Boudreau sold cheap liquor and handled fixes downtown, and sometimes hot goods. Hooker put his beer down and looked at Eirie. "How's the chin?"

Eirie touched the scab and smiled. "I'll make it."

"Well," Hooker said, "what's on for tomorrow? How about tryin' downtown a while?"

He waited, looking from one to the other. There was no response. "Hey, c'mon, you guys." He laughed. "You takin' a vacation or something? What's goin' on?"

Luther smiled and looked at him. "Yeah," he said, "that's about it, Johnny. That's what I wanted to talk to you about. I'm quitting."

"You're what?"

"Quitting. Retiring."

Hooker felt like his heart had jumped out of its moorings and dropped into his stomach. Luther quitting? "Whatd'ya mean? What're you gonna do?"

"Oh, I don't know," Luther said. "I got a brother in

the freight business down in K.C. Maybe I'll buy in with him. It ain't too exciting, but it's legal."

He was serious. Hooker couldn't believe it. Con men never retired.

Eirie didn't look surprised. He was still gazing sleepily at the table. Luther must have told him about it earlier.

"Yeah," Luther said, "I'm in pretty good shape after today. An' I'm movin' along in years. Maybe I'll just go back to Mississippi an' sit in the sun." He smiled. "Just sit an' watch the white folks work."

"Jesus," Hooker said. He shook his head and sat back in his chair. He didn't know what to think.

"Hey." Luther laughed. "Straighten up, huh? Things ain't that bad. It's time you been movin' up anyway."

"Movin' up to what?"

"Big con."

Big con was peddling phony oil stocks to millionaires and bilking widows out of their fortunes. Hooker had never been much interested in it.

"Yeah," Luther said, "you're too good for this nickel-and-dime street conning, Johnny. Ya been wastin' your time. I shoulda sent you up a long time ago." He pulled a slip of paper out of his pocket and tossed it across the table. "You go see that guy. He can teach ya everything you gotta know."

The paper said "Henry Gondorff," with an address scrawled under it. Hooker read it and looked up. "Jesus, Luther, you taught me everything I know."

"Yeah, an' I ain't got nothin' more to teach ya. Ya know more than I do. I wouldn't turn ya out if you weren't ready." He stood up and pulled a handful of change from his pocket, dropping coins on the table.

Hooker looked at the slip of paper again, not knowing what to say. Jesus, three years, he thought. "Hey, look," he said, "if I see this guy, and if something works out, you'll take a cut, won't ya?"

Luther smiled and shook his head. "I'm out, Johnny."

"If that's the way you want it."

"That's the way I want it." He waved at Eirie and gave Hooker a chuck on the chin as he moved off in the crowd.

Where the hell was the dame, Joe Mottola suddenly wondered. She was behind him a minute ago. But now the whole room was whirling, and he couldn't see her. He quickly grabbed the hat-check counter to keep his balance, and twisted his head. Ah, yes, there she was, behind him.

"Come on, Joe," the girl said, "lift your arm."

She was holding his coat for him. A nice girl. A pretty blond girl. Mottola lifted his hand from the counter, but quickly grabbed it again as he felt himself falling.

"Try the other arm first," the girl said.

Yes, that was a better idea. He got the left arm in, then turned so he could balance himself with the left hand, and slipped the right arm in. Jesus, he was drunk. But he would be all right once he got the girl to her room. Even drunk, he was good in bed. Did he have any money to tip the hat-check girl? He had borrowed ten bucks this afternoon, and he remembered breaking the ten about three hours ago. He fumbled in his pockets.

"That's all right." The hat-check girl smiled. "Forget it."

"Much obliged," Mottola said. The words came out in one slurring syllable, and the blond was shoving him toward the door.

The fresh night air felt good. Mottola stopped for a moment, taking a deep breath. He felt the girl's grip tighten on his arm, and he saw the fancy-uniformed doorman rushing toward him. Mottola lifted his free hand, planted it in the doorman's chest and shoved hard. "Don-tush-me, sombitch," he said. Then he was plummeting forward toward the open door of a taxi. Three more steps, two, one, he made it, tumbling headlong into the back seat. He made it, he told himself happily. His hand slipped from the seat. He planted it again, and climbed numbly into a sitting position. Where was the girl? There she was, standing outside the cab. Why wasn't she getting in? Mottola squinted at her. He saw the blurry form lean forward, blow him a kiss, and turn back toward the nightclub. What the hell, he thought. He had spent every dime he had on the dumb dame.

He grabbed the door for support and took one long step onto the sidewalk. But then somebody had his arm. It was a man, and he was twisting his wrist up behind him, forcing him back into the cab. "What the hell you doing?" Mottola asked mushily.

The man dropped to the seat beside him. Another man jumped in on the other side, and both doors slammed.

"This's my cab," Mottola said.

"Shut up," the man on his left muttered. "The lake front," he said to the driver.

Mottola looked at each of the men, at their hard, expressionless faces under the black fedoras. He swallowed hard. He closed his eyes and dropped his head back, letting his mind go numb, hoping to God he would pass out quickly. He had heard people make cracks about that long garbage chute at the back of the cannery. They said there were more bodies down there at the bottom of the lake with cement shoes than there was garbage. He had laughed at the cracks.

"I didn't take the money," Mottola blurted out in desperation.

"Shut up," the man on his right said. He turned abruptly, and Mottola's head snapped back as the heavy pistol butt cracked against his forehead. He was out.

It was cold when Hooker and Eirie came out of Boudreau's. There were a few solitary lights burning in the early-morning mist, but the street was empty.

Hooker turned up his collar and hunched his shoulders against the chill. He still couldn't get over Luther's quitting. And he felt bad about the way it had ended. He would probably see the old man again sometime. But he should have shaken his hand, or said thanks, or good-bye, or something. He shook his head.

"I was hustlin' pinball down at Gianelli's when I met Luther. A buck and a half was a good day for me back then."

Eirie smiled. "You'll be makin' big money now."

"Aw, I don't need anything more than I got."

"You ain't gonna have nothin' if you don't lay off them games of chance. There's a depression on, ya know."

"There's always a depression on."

"Yeah, but if you saved a little, you wouldn't have to grift so much."

"I like griftin'."

"You could buy yourself some things. Clothes, or a nice car."

"I don't look any good in clothes, and I don't know how to drive. What else ya got to sell, Eirie?"

Eirie heard it first. It was the scrape of a trash can just inside the alley they were passing. He turned, and then he was staring, petrified, at the two shadows coming at them.

It all happened so fast that Hooker had no time to think. For an instant he froze. Then he whirled and headed out into the street at full speed. But he knew it was too late. The man was almost on top of him the minute he turned. There was a grab at his arm, and two strides into the street he felt his legs clamped together. Suddenly he was slammed to the concrete.

It was all over that quickly. Hooker lay stunned for a moment, trying to collect his senses. Then he felt the arms release him.

"Okay, Hooker, on your feet!"

He knew the voice. He got up slowly and brushed the dust from his suit. The man in front of him was short and stocky, wearing a heavy topcoat, his hat brim half-covering his eyes. Detective Lieutenant Raymond Snyder.

"Move!" the voice barked. Snyder grabbed him roughly at the back of the collar and gave him a shove. Hooker moved. He also knew what was coming. It was Snyder's weekly shakedown, Hooker's dues for being permitted to work the streets.

In the darkness of the alley another plainclothes cop was holding a gun on Eirie.

Hooker smiled. "Things a little slow down at the bunco department, Snyder? Somebody lose the dominoes?"

It was a mistake. Snyder was in no mood for humor. He smiled coldly. Then his hand shot out, grabbed Hooker's shirt front, and shoved, slamming him against the wall.

"Hooker," he said tightly, "you scored blood money today. You need a friend."

"Go roll yourself a shoplifter," Hooker said. The hand was still gripping his shirt, Hooker pushed it roughly aside.

Mistake number two. A knee came up and drove like a sledgehammer into his groin. Hooker gasped, doubling sharply forward with the pain. He grabbed himself, clenched his teeth against the fiery ache, and sucked in air. Then the left side of his head exploded, and he was suddenly clattering headlong into empty garbage cans. He stumbled, reached out for empty air, and hit solid ground.

"Take it easy, Snyder," he heard Eirie say from miles away. Then there was silence.

With his right ear against the cold concrete, Hooker breathed deeply, hoping feebly that this was the end of it, and Snyder would go away. But then he saw Snyder's black shoes appear next to his face. He slowly maneuvered a hand under himself and pushed into a sitting position.

"You got the wrong guy," Hooker said hoarsely. "I

been home all day with the flu." He gave Snyder a weak smile and struggled halfway up to his feet. "You can stake out my toilet if ya want."

Again he felt Snyder's hand at his shirt front, and once more he was jammed against the wall, Snyder's face close to his. Snyder's breath smelled of bourbon and peppermint.

"I'll tell you what you did, smart boy," he said. "You tied into a loaded mark on Forty-seventh, across from Maxie's. You and Coleman played the switch on him and blew him off to a cab. If the kid hadn't been a numbers runner, it woulda been perfect."

Hooker gazed impassively back at him. Inside, his heart dropped a beat. Luther's initial fear had been right; the eleven grand *was* racket money.

"Gotcha worried, huh, Hooker?" Snyder said with a laugh. "Well, I'm tellin' you, kid, you got somethin' to worry about."

"Are you crazy?" Hooker snorted. "I'm not stupid enough to play for racket money."

"Not intentionally, maybe. But that don't make no difference to Amon Lorrimer. He'll swat you like a fly."

Hooker shrugged. "I'll square it with a fixer." He wondered who Amon Lorrimer was. But it didn't make much difference. Nobody lifted eleven grand from a runner and lived to talk about it. Jesus, Hooker thought, he had to tell Luther. They'd go for him first.

Snyder was smiling, shaking his head. "No fixer in the world can buy you a prayer. Not if I put the finger on you." He let go of the shirt, and Hooker leaned heavily against the wall. Snyder would name his price now, and Hooker would pay it.

Snyder glanced over at Eirie. He pulled at his nose a couple of times and looked back at Hooker. "The way I figure it," he said, "your end of the score was at least five G's. I want three, no matter what it was."

Hooker shook his head. "My end was only two."

"Isn't that too bad? Now you're gonna have to dig up another grand somewhere, ain't you?"

Hooker looked at him. Snyder was in no mood to bargain. And with Hooker's days numbered, Snyder would not be interested in promises. "All right," Hooker said. He reached deep through his pocket and into the lining of his coat. His hand came out with a thick bundle of money, and he handed it over. In the darkness, Snyder could not examine it too closely. The detective grabbed the bundle, spun quickly through the bills, and smiled.

"You're a smart egg, Hooker. No use dying for three grand, huh?"

Snyder turned and motioned to his partner. He shoved the money inside his coat, and they both hustled off down the alley.

Hooker watched them for a moment and then moved toward the street. He remembered seeing a phone booth half a block back.

"Come on, Eirie," he yelled, breaking into a run. "We gotta get word to Luther, fast."

Luther had left Boudreau's an hour and a half ago. He had been home for at least an hour. But Hooker pushed the thought from his mind as he ran. They couldn't possibly get to him that fast. At the phone booth he banged open the door and fished in his pockets for a nickel as Eirie skidded to a stop behind him.

"Where the hell'd you get that money?" Eirie shouted. "I thought you blew it."

"I did," Hooker said. He found a nickel and dropped it in the slot. "That stuff was counterfeit."

"What?" Eirie screamed. "Are you crazy? As soon as he finds out that's funny money, he'll rush his finger right to Lorrimer. Jesus, Hooker, you're committing suicide!"

"What difference does it make? If Snyder knows we grabbed that money, so does everybody else. Snyder never gets anything first."

He had finished dialing, now and was unconsciously counting the rings, praying for them to stop, and for Luther's voice to come on. But the rattling buzz was followed only by silence. Hooker's hopes sank. "There's no answer," he said grimly to Eirie.

"Maybe he didn't go home."

"Yeah," Hooker said, not believing it. He banged the receiver back and looked out at the empty street. Jesus, if they got Luther ... He didn't know what he'd do.

"Listen to me, Hooker," Eirie was saying, "Whatever you do, don't go back to your room tonight. You understand? Don't go anyplace you usually go. Get outa town, or something."

Hooker was not listening. He moved past Eirie and began walking numbly up the street, trying to think. They couldn't have gotten Luther. Luther was too smart to be taken by a couple dumb torpedoes. He was suspicious about the money. He would have been careful.

"Hooker!" Eirie shouted, but he was too far behind. Hooker was running now, racing blindly down the street, past dark stores and across empty intersections. He was in the black district, and then he was on Huron Street, and he saw Luther's apartment building ahead.

There was the stagnant odor of garbage and bad toilets that all tenements had. Hooker took the steps four at a time up to the dimly lighted third floor. He would tell Luther. Luther would throw something in a bag, and they would get out of town tonight. They could catch a freight. Or they would walk if they had to. Hooker spotted Luther's room noticed that the door was half open. Without hesitating, he whirled around the door frame and banged the door all the way open. Then he stopped short.

The room was empty. A lamp was lying sideways in a chair, its bulb still burning. Another chair lay on its side, and the grounds from a toppled coffeepot were strewn on the carpet. Hooker looked around slowly, his breath coming in shallow gasps. He stared over at the window. It was open, the curtains stirring gently from the breeze.

He moved forward, stepping around the coffeepot to the window. He had to bend forward and thrust his head out to see anything below.

A single lightbulb burned in the tiny courtyard three stories down. A clothesline from the flat just beneath him had been broken and was dangling freely. At the end of it, Luther's body lay motionless, one leg doubled under him, an elbow protruding awkwardly upward, and the right side of his head jammed grotesquely into a bloody pool on the concrete.

Hooker drew back numbly from the window and slowly closed it. He rested his arm on the cross-brace, leaned his forehead against it, and closed his eyes. "God damn," he groaned in hopeless, silent frustration.

It was his fault Luther was dead. He had picked the mark this morning. He had brushed aside Luther's fears about where the money had come from. And he'd blown the four thousand dollars with no concern for the consequences.

Spasms of sobbing rose from his stomach, clogging his throat as he tried to hold back the tears.

II. The Setup

1

Hooker could see no cops or railroad detectives around. There was a steady stream of people hurrying to catch trains, and others coming the opposite direction carrying bags, heading for the taxi stands outside.

Hooker scanned the lobby, looking for a man, any man who was alone and looked like he might have some money in his pocket.

He had cleaned himself up as best he could in the men's room. But his suit was dirty and wrinkled, and he had lost his tie somewhere. He had been keeping out of sight for the past two days, doing a little panhandling to buy food, sticking mostly to the alleys or the black district, where Lorrimer's hoods were not likely to find him. He had slept in a produce warehouse the first night. This morning he had been awakened in an alley by a cop whacking the bottoms of his feet with a nightstick. He tried some panhandling again, but then decided to hell with it. He was a con man. He would get some money conning, and then he would go see the guy Luther had told him about. He couldn't spend the rest of his life digging in garbage cans. If they were going to get him, they were going to get him.

"Chicago Northwestern leaving track six for Seattle in ten minutes," the loudspeaker droned. "All aboard, please."

Hooker walked slowly across the lobby toward the big board listing arrivals and departures, and then stopped, watching a gray-haired man with a briefcase. It was a possibility. The guy was about fifty, wearing steel-rimmed glasses, and he didn't seem to be in a hurry. Hooker moved forward. He adopted a grim, businesslike manner and pulled out his wallet.

"Excuse me, sir. Treasury Department. I'd like to ask you a few questions."

The man gasped, looking only briefly at the badge in the wallet, and Hooker quickly put it away. Hooker had lifted the badge in the toy department of Woolworth's on the way to the station.

"What's the matter?" the man said. "I haven't done anything."

"We don't doubt that," Hooker said briskly. "But there's a counterfeiting operation passing money in the station. Have you made any purchases here today?"

"Well ... I ... yes. I bought a small gift. And I had a sandwich in the coffee shop."

"Then I'm afraid we'll have to impound your money until we're sure it's all good. Can I see your wallet, please?"

The man blinked a couple of times, then handed over the wallet. "But I've got a train to catch."

Hooker pulled out two twenties and a ten. "It'll only take twenty minutes or so. Then you can pick it up at the window down the hall." He gestured vaguely toward the hall running to the men's room.

The man looked more closely at him now, at his unshaven face and rumpled suit. He was having doubts, but he didn't know what to say. "What about all these other people?" he finally asked.

Hooker gave him a sharp look, as if suddenly irritated. "We'll get 'em! Give us a chance. I'm not the only agent in here, you know. If we go around advertising ourselves, how many counterfeiters do you think we're gonna catch?" As if all the frustrations of his long vigilance had finally brought him to the boiling point, Hooker angrily grabbed at his own tattered suit. "You think I'm wearing this rag here 'cause I like it? Christ, everybody thinks life's a holiday or something when you got a badge. Listen, I been here since three this morning, Charlie, and I never knew there was so much ugliness in people. You try to help 'em, and they spit on you. I should have let you go and gotten yourself arrested for passing false notes."

The man was thoroughly taken aback by the outburst. "I'm sorry," he said, "I really am. I don't mean to give you any trouble. But I can't wait for twenty minutes. My train leaves in ten."

Hooker sighed impatiently. He glanced off at the ticket lines and the people rushing to catch trains, and then back. "All right," he said, "I'll give you a break." He pointed toward the hall again. "Down that hall there's an office, third door on the left. Go in there and wait at the window." He glanced suspiciously at the money in his hand. "I'll take this in the back and run it through right away. We'll have you out of here in a couple of minutes."

The man smiled with relief. "Thank you. You don't know how much I appreciate this."

"It's okay. I don't mind helping out an honest citizen."

"Thanks again," the man said, and headed for the third door on the left. He strode on through only to find himself face to face with a wall of flushing urinals.

Hooker sprinted off toward the back of the station.

Once out of the lobby, he shoved the money in his pocket, went out a side door, and headed for the waterfront.

The address on the crumpled slip of paper Luther had given him was a barnlike two-story building at the end of the amusement-park boardwalk. The place looked tilted, like it was going to topple into the lake at any minute. The lower section enclosed a battered carrousel with a heavy steel grating pulled across the front. The upper floor had four curtained windows that might be rooms or a couple of apartments. An outside wooden staircase ran up to a door at the back.

Hooker looked around at the building for a long time, and then saw a woman come out the door and start down the stairs. She was about thirty-five, a tough-looking dame with flaming red hair. She had an apple in one hand and was clutching an old flannel robe with the other, moving carefully down the steps on what looked like high-heeled slippers. Hooker watched until she picked up the morning paper and turned to go back up.

"Excuse me," he said. "I'm looking for a guy named Henry Gondorff. You know him?"

"Never heard of him."

"You sure?"

She had opened the paper, studying the headlines as she moved up the stairs. "Get lost."

"Luther Coleman sent me."

The woman stopped. "You Hooker?"

"Yes."

She sighed and started down again. "Why the hell didn't you say so?" She came down to a small door at the side of the building and pulled some keys from her pocket. "Christ, I thought maybe you were a copper or something." She gave him a quick once-over as she pushed the door open. "I'm Billie. Henry wasn't expecting you so soon. It's the room over there in back of the merry-go-round."

The place was eerie in the shadows of the late afternoon. Huge painted horses pranced motionless in the shadows above him. Hooker shoved his hands in his back pockets and glanced up at them as he moved around to the door in the far corner. He knocked softly. This was a hell of a place to live. But he had seen worse.

He knocked again, more firmly this time, and then tried the door. It was not locked.

"Gondorff?" He stuck his head inside. He was about to call again, when he noticed a pair of stockinged feet protruding from behind the bed. His eyes followed them along the floor to a large snoring head although there was considerable flesh in between. A dozen gold inlays revealed themselves as the sleeping figure inhaled. Then the mouth closed a little, the lips smacked and snorted and rattled, and the air whistled out. Then came the long, squealing inhale, with another display of gold.

Hooker sighed heavily. Books, magazines, dirty clothes, empty beer bottles, and cigar butts were strewn over the bed and into the tiny bathroom in the corner. The dresser drawers were all askew, clothes dangling from each of them. An empty bourbon bottle stood on top. And drunk as a skunk, lying flat on his back was the great Henry Gondorff.

Luther Coleman must have been out of his goddamned mind.

With Lieutenant Snyder and Amon Lorrimer's goons searching for him, it seemed doubtful that this old sot would be of any help. On the other hand, Hooker had no place else to go.

The alcoholic stench in the room was suffocating. He moved around Gondorff, stepped over the debris, and pried open the small window above the bed. He glanced at the small stall shower in the bathroom, and then stood indecisively over the snoring body. Should he undress him first? Gondorff looked like he weighed over two hundred pounds.

To hell with it, Hooker thought. He moved to the side of the bed, picked up the man's limp right arm, hooked it around his own neck, and lifted.

The snoring stopped. Gondorff gurgled and mumbled a little as Hooker hoisted him to his feet and maneuvered him toward the shower.

It took three or four minutes to bring him around. Gondorff brushed sleepily at the water. Then his eyes popped open, and he gasped for breath, trying to shield the icy stream from his head. He struggled to get himself off the shower floor, but then gave it up.

"Turn the goddamned thing off, will ya?" The voice boomed out of the shower like an angry bull elephant.

Hooker sat on the bed and smiled. There was still some life in the old bastard.

"For Christ's sake," Gondorff roared, "you tryin' to drown me?" He struggled again. He reached up for the faucet handles, but was a foot short.

"Goddamnit!" he sputtered. "Turn it off!"

"You sober?"

"What the hell d'ya mean, am I sober? I can talk, can't I?"

"Then turn it off yourself."

Gondorff stared at him, blinking away the water. He muttered to himself, rolled to the side, lifted himself on one knee, and twisted the faucet shut. He dropped back to his sitting position and sat breathing heavily. "Hooker?"

"Yeah."

The big man looked down at his wet clothes and sighed. "Glad to meet ya, kid. You're a real horse's ass."

"I wouldn't be hangin' around here if I had anyplace else to go. I've seen drunks before."

"Yeah," Gondorff said. He wiped his face and shook the water from his hand. "I'm sorry about Luther."

"He had you down as a big-timer. What happened?"

Gondorff ignored the sneering tone. He shrugged

easily. "Aw, I conned a senator from Florida on a stocks deal. A real lop-ear." He smiled. "The dope thought he was gonna take over General Electric. Then some Memphis chantoozie woke him up, and he put the feds on me." He shrugged again. "I lammed it around for a while ... Philly, Savannah, Baltimore. Nothin' towns. Looks like it's cooled off now, though."

"Ya played the big con since?"

"No," he said. He climbed to his feet and looked over the damage to his clothes. "I still know how, though."

Hooker watched him, wondering if the old man really knew his game anymore. He had his doubts.

"You had anything to eat?" Gondorff asked.

"Yeah, I picked something up."

Gondorff dropped his suspenders and pulled off his shirt. "Lorrimer after ya?"

"I don't know. I haven't seen anybody."

"Ya never do, kid." He pushed the bathroom door shut.

Five minutes later he came out, and dressed himself. The transformation was dramatic. From a broken-down bum he turned into what looked like a retired sportsman on his way to Florida for the winter. He put on a narrow bow tie, and then a pale plaid jacket and neatly pressed pants. Gondorff talked, and Hooker listened.

The carrousel out front, Gondorff told him, didn't make much money. It was a front for the girlie house Billie ran upstairs. "Great little countess, that Billie," he said, brushing his hair. "Learned the business out at Al Capone's Maple Inn in Forest View. That was before your time, I guess. But Billie's got a few friends around." He laughed. "You gotta have friends in that business. If you don't, Mr. Luciano suggests you look for some other line of work. You meet Billie?"

"Yeah."

"This town ain't what it used to be." He found a

clean pair of socks in the rubble of the dresser and sat down in the chair. "Since they chilled Capone, there's a lot of newcomers trying to muscle in. Ya gotta be careful. Ya don't wanta get tangled up with any of those people." He glanced at Hooker and smiled. "I knew a guy back in twenty-eight who had a good play goin' for a hundred grand in phony stock. The day he was gonna make the sting, he found out the mark was Jack McGurn. Know who he was?"

"No."

Gondorff chuckled softly. "Machine Gun Jack McGurn, they called him. One of Capone's trigger men. He liked to cut people in half with bullets. That kind of people ya don't wanta do business with. Ya know what I mean?"

Hooker nodded. He suspected Gondorff's meaning was broader than it appeared. Gondorff knew Luther had been killed by Lorrimer. And he probably knew why.

"Yeah." Gondorff smiled. "Racketeers and feds. They're bad business for people like us. But we live and learn, huh? Come on, I'll show ya around."

Hooker followed him out to the carrousel. Gondorff moved slowly around the machine, checking straps and poles, shaking the horses to see if any were loose. "Luther said you were a smart kid. Think you're smart enough to run a merry-go-round?"

Hooker had no idea what the question meant, or how to answer it. Apparently Gondorff expected no answer. He looked up at Billie, who suddenly appeared on the mezzanine above the carrousel.

"You feelin' all right today, Henry?" she shouted.

"Fine, Billie."

Billie too had undergone a transformation. The dumpy flannel robe had been replaced by a tight-fitting yellow silk dress, and her red hair was neatly combed. At least from a distance she looked ten years younger. "You mind opening the round a little early?"

she asked, struggling with an earring. "We got some business coming in before hours."

Gondorff waved okay. She disappeared, and he moved on, busying himself with the equipment again.

Hooker wondered if he was being tested somehow, if the old man's stories and questions were designed to put him off balance. Gondorff had found a loose pole now, and peered into the darkness under the platform.

"Gondorff," Hooker said, "Luther told me to talk to you about learnin' big con."

The old man squinted up at the greasy gears at the top of the machine. "You don't act much like you want to learn it."

"I wanta make a play for Amon Lorrimer."

Gondorff looked at him and smiled. "You do, huh. You don't know nothin' about big con, and you don't know nothin' about Amon Lorrimer, but you want to make a play for him. You got a great sense of humor, kid. I'll say that for ya."

"I know he killed Luther."

"Yeah, and he's killed a lot of other people too. But their friends got brains enough to keep away from him."

"You afraid of him?"

Gondorff laughed again. He shook his head and moved over to the carrousel controls. "Yeah, I'm afraid of him. I'm just a con man, kid, not the U.S. Marines. Do you know who Lorrimer is?"

"I know he runs the numbers on the South Side."

"Yeah. An' he runs half the politicians in Chicago and New York. An' a string of banks, an' a cannery, an' four or five protection rackets, an' fifty or so New York trigger men." He laughed again. "How much were ya figurin' on playin' him for?"

"I don't know. How much has he got?"

"You really got this all figured out, haven't ya? Jesus, Luther told me you were smart. Why don't ya ask Lorrimer for a financial report?"

"You're not interested, huh?"

Gondorff hit one of the control levers, then slapped it back when nothing happened. "It ain't a case of bein' interested, kid. Listen, if you figure on conning a man like Lorrimer, you can't just take his money and then laugh it off. Most people, they get taken an' they feel like assholes. They don't go to the cops, 'cause they don't want the cops or anybody else to know how stupid they been. But a guy like Lorrimer don't need no cops. He's got his own law-enforcement business. You know what I mean? For him it's just a phone call, an' you're stuffed in a garbage can with your throat leakin' all over the bottom."

Gondorff sighed and tinkered with the controls. "You con someone like Lorrimer, you got to keep his con long after you've stung him. You'd have to do it so's he'd never even know he was conned. That's tough to do."

Hooker smiled to himself. The wheels were turning in the old man's head.

"An' you'd need plenty a good men," Gondorff said, "a first-class mob."

"You know anybody who'd do it?"

Gondorff scratched his head. "There's some guys around."

Hooker waited while the old man thought about it. "Whatd'ya think?"

"Jesus," Gondorff said. "Amon Lorrimer. It'd be the con of the century, wouldn't it?"

2

Amon Lorrimer arrived at his Wall Street office a little after one o'clock. He had spent most of the morning at the bank in Jersey going over the books with the manager and chief accountant. From the bank he and Joe Leonard had gone back to town, had a steam bath and lunch at the club, and then driven to the financial district.

There were three accountants and two attorneys waiting for him.

The bank in Jersey had two big loan defaults, both from building contractors. They were enough to break the bank, and under normal circumstances the simplest thing to do was eat the loss, throw the corporation into bankruptcy and fold the bank. But considering the fact that more than half of the bank's assets were phony deposits from Lorrimer's numbers profits, there were complications. In a bankruptcy proceeding, the federal bank examiners would be all over the place. And there would be the questions about federal insurance for the depositors. This would throw too much light on the character and financing of the bank.

As far as Lorrimer was concerned, it was all bullshit, and he sat back and listened to the proposals and arguments with half-closed eyes. Since the FBI had gone after the rackets for income-tax evasion, the problem of hiding money and disguising it as legitimate business profits had become a pain in the ass. It had not only forced him to hire an army of high-priced accountants and attorneys, and it provided opportunities for wise guys, like the loan officer in the New Jersey bank, to scrape off big chunks of the profits.

The loan officer had taken off for Mexico three days ago. It was his sudden departure that had prompted them to take a look at the books. And it had taken only five minutes to find out that the two contracting companies were phony. The man had set it up three months ago—maybe with some help from Lorrimer's enemies—and the cash had gone out in four big payments for nonexistent construction jobs.

They would get the son-of-a-bitch. They'd already traced him down to New Orleans and then Mexico City, and it would be only a matter of days before they caught up with him. But whether or not they could get the money back was another question. And the money represented two months of income from the numbers.

Lorrimer looked impatiently at the circle of men seated in front of him. He was getting sick of lawyer talk and bookkeepers with pockets full of pencils.

What he needed was one big haul, a million or two cash, so he could dump all these people and get the hell out of the country. Either that or knock a few more heads so people would quit getting ideas.

Joe Leonard slipped into the room. He waited by the door for a minute, and then mouthed something, indicating there was some urgent private business to be discussed.

Lorrimer came forward in his chair. "All right," he said. "You guys get this settled tonight. Either we close the fuckin' place and burn up the records, or we figure a way to pump in more money. But I want it done tomorrow, and I want it done right."

They all nodded and smiled and gathered their briefcases. They assured him with their ten-thousand-dollar-a-year smiles that everything would be taken care of, and then filed out. Leonard closed the door and took a seat next to the desk.

"I just talked to Hunt," he said. "He says Moran doesn't want to talk to you. He wants five hundred grand, and that's it."

"He's crazy. Who's got five hundred grand?"

"He says they got it on the North Side, and if you don't want to deal, they will."

"Bullshit."

"I don't know," Leonard said doubtfully.

"Yeah, you don't know," Lorrimer said. "But I do. If Moran goes along with Schultz or Nitti, they'll cut his throat and take back the cash in twenty-four hours."

"Probably. And we could do the same thing. We oughta think about it, Amon."

Lorrimer nodded and thought about it.

The city of New York, along with Jersey and Philadelphia and some outlying areas, were roughly divided into five territories. The mobs in the three north and western territories had been fighting with each other for the last six months, and now the battle was spilling over into Moran's and Lorrimer's areas. Lorrimer had proposed to Moran that they get together and fight back. But now Moran wanted half a million to form an alliance. He was a stupid son-of-a-bitch, a cheap whore who would end up getting his head blown off if he ever got the cash. But it looked like an all-out gang war was coming, and something had to be done.

"How's it look with Nitti?" Lorrimer asked. Nitti's territory adjoined Lorrimer's, and he was taking the brunt of the invasions. Four of his numbers spots had been hit in the last week.

"He's in trouble."

"Think it's worth helping him?"

Leonard shook his head doubtfully. "If we had Moran with us, we'd have the muscle. Otherwise ..." He shrugged.

It was interesting, Lorrimer thought. He had talked to each of the warring mob leaders and they all denied any ambitions to muscle in on the others. He knew they were all lying, and they were all pulling in more troops from all over the country.

"You think Moran would take less?"

"Hunt says no. Moran's been blowin' his money for five years now, and he's broke."

"Everybody's broke."

"Yeah, but I'd think about it, Amon."

"Why?"

"If we could swing it, we take over Moran's organization. Then we move in and save Nitti's ass. That puts you on top of the whole thing. Then you're in a position to deal tough with the other two. You could have the whole town wrapped up. And Moran gets a ride down to the river."

Lorrimer smiled at the last statement. Giving Moran a long look at the sandy bottom was the most attractive part of the idea. But getting five hundred grand in cash to start the ball rolling was another question. And if he did it, he would have to act fast. Buy Moran, throw Moran's goons behind Nitti, and blast a couple of dozen North Side spots all at the same time. It could be done. Lorrimer thought about it and nodded.

"Stall him," he said. "Call Hunt and tell him the idea sounds pretty good to us. Tell him we're thinking about it, and we'll let him know." Lorrimer smiled. "And tell him to give my best to Moran."

"Right." Leonard smiled. He got up and headed for the door.

Lorrimer propped a foot on a drawer and eased back. "Hey," he said, "you get that business settled in Chicago?"

"Most of it."

"Whatd'ya mean, 'most of it'?"

"Mottola's in the lake, and Garule got the colored guy."

"Yeah, I saw that in the paper. But you said there were two of 'em."

"We're still looking for the other one. We'll get him."

"Who you usin'?"

"Riley and Cole."

"Why two?"

"This one's gonna be harder." Leonard smiled. "He probably knows we're lookin' for him."

"I thought you said he was a punk grifter."

"Yeah, but he might have a bug up his ass. He and the nigger were pretty close."

Lorrimer nodded. "All right. But I don't want any heat from this. You tell those guys to rig it like an accident, and make sure they get rid of the body. Garule never shoulda left that black ape layin' around like that."

"Right," Leonard said.

Hooker saw very little of Gondorff in the next three days. The old man dressed up like the ambassador to England, and hustled off down the boardwalk each morning. He returned in the late afternoon to crank up the carrousel and direct traffic up to Billie's frolic rooms on the mezzanine.

"Relax, kid," he told Hooker. "Things are coming together. One thing you gotta learn in big con is patience. In two or three days you're gonna learn more than you ever wanted to know about the confidence racket."

"How long before we hit him?" Hooker asked.

Gondorff laughed. "You really hate that guy, don't ya? Don't worry about it. It'll take maybe a week after we get started."

Billie fixed breakfast for him after Gondorff left in the morning. He ate it in the small kitchen behind her bar while she read the morning paper. She discouraged conversation, never lifting her eyes from the paper as she answered his questions.

"How long you known Gondorff?" Hooker asked the first morning.

"Ten, fifteen years."

"Is he good?"

"He knows it all, sweetie."

"You think he can still handle himself?"

"Ask him."

"Does he drink much?"

She smiled at that. She glanced at him and returned to the paper with a shrug. "How much is much?"

That was about all he got out of Billie. He returned to his room and waited. The one thing you gotta learn, Gondorff had said, is patience. Hooker began to have doubts about his future in big con.

On the afternoon of the third day, Gondorff came

back smiling. "All set," he said. "Now, we have to get you in shape. Get your coat, and let's go."

In the cab Gondorff told him there would be three more people involved in the play for Lorrimer—Kid Twist, Eddie Niles, and J. J. Singleton. The names meant nothing to Hooker. The cab stopped on Michigan Avenue, and Gondorff marched him into the back of a fancy haberdashery.

"Something in gray, I think, Alex," Gondorff said to the manager. "Not too flashy."

"Certainly, Mr. Gondorff," the man said. He brought out three suits. Gondorff chose the two most conservative ones, and Hooker stood patiently while the man tugged and shifted and put chalk marks on them. He tried on shoes and socks and shirts and ties, and the man promised everything would be ready the next day.

Gondorff enjoyed Hooker's transformation far more than Hooker did. In the barber shop down the street the old man hovered over the barber directing every snip of the scissors, and an hour later Hooker walked out with a new comb, a hairbrush, and a bottle of after-shave lotion.

The next stop wasn't as classy as the first two—an inexpensive apartment house on Newberry Street. While Gondorff waited in the cab, Hooker rented a small room furnished with a bed, table, and sink. Hooker paid a week's rent in advance, and the cab returned them to the amusement park.

The three men who comprised Gondorff's hastily assembled mob were waiting in Billie's parlor when they got back. Gondorff waited until they had all crowded into the small storage room upstairs before he introduced Hooker.

Of the three men, only J. J. Singleton had the appearance of a typical confidence man. He was about fifty-five, with silky gray hair, and a beaming, red-faced smile. He was wearing spats and a neatly pressed suit. He shook Hooker's hand as if he was a long-lost child. "Pleased to meet you, son. A real pleasure. I've heard some fine things about you. Wonderful things." Hooker smiled. He could imagine Singleton going on with the routine, putting his arm around his shoulders and telling him about a wonderful investment opportunity, a chance to get in on the ground floor of America's fastest-growing industry.

Kid Twist was a tall, slender, impeccably dressed man about thirty-five, with a youthful, outdoor smile on his tanned face. There was a classiness about him that suggested tennis, bridge, and yachting.

Eddie Niles, on the other hand, seemed to have a permanent scowl on his lined face. He was probably in his early fifties, but he looked older. He acknowledged the introduction with a curt nod and found himself a chair.

Gondorff locked the door as they all pulled themselves up to the table in the center of the room. He took off his coat, hooked it on a nail, and looked at Twist as he rolled up his sleeves. "Okay," he said, "how'd you make out, Kid?"

Kid Twist carefully balanced his cigarette on the edge of an ashtray. He drew three photographs from his inside pocket. "These," he said, glancing at the pictures and passing them along, "are Lorrimer's favorite torpedoes. Riley, Garule, and Cole." He smiled over at Hooker, and Hooker stiffened a little as Twist went on. "Those guys do most of the small jobs. But Lorrimer might not want to use them on you. They're kind of messy." He gave a short laugh. "No class."

Hooker nodded faintly. He hadn't expected the discussion to start out on himself. He tried to look casually at each of the pictures as they arrived.

"We've got reason to believe Garule was the guy who hit Luther," Twist continued, "so they probably won't send him after you. But if you see one of these other two, find yourself a crowd and get lost. Or take 'em someplace you know you can handle them."

Gondorff had settled into the chair next to Hooker

now. "But most of all," he said, "you let us know. If they got a hit on you, we'll have to fold up the con. You're too exposed. You got that?"

Hooker felt all four pairs of eyes on him. He knew damn well Lorrimer had a hit out on him. If he didn't before, he'd certainly been fingered by Snyder, and the word had gone out by now. But he couldn't tell Gondorff about Snyder. He nodded and looked at Twist. "You sure it'll be one of these two?"

Twist gave him a wry smile. "No. They're just the only ones we know."

There wasn't much comfort in that.

"All right," Gondorff said, closing the matter, "anybody got any ideas?"

Singleton shook his head. "Lorrimer's a fast egg, Henry. He's not gonna sit still for any standard play."

"Everybody'll sit still for something. Even Lorrimer must get hungry once in a while. What'd you find out about the rattler, Eddie?"

Eddie Niles looked up. "He's been taking the Century Limited outa New York on Tuesdays. He gets into Chicago the next day. He usually stays here till Thursday to check his policy operations, and then flies back that night."

Gondorff nodded thoughtfully. "A day and a night on the train."

"Yeah. The porters say he runs a braced card game in his car both nights. Hundred-dollar minimum, straight poker." Niles's mouth twisted a little—the closest Hooker had seen him come to a smile. "Last time he pulled in here, he was fifteen grand heavier than when he left New York."

"Fancies himself a gambler, huh?"

"Lotta plungers ride that train just to play him."

Gondorff looked at Singleton and smiled. "See, J. J., he's slowin' down already."

Hooker listened as they discussed the style and habits of Lorrimer's poker playing. Most of it was in gambler's shorthand, and he didn't follow it too closely. He wondered if it was going to be that simple, if they intended to clean Lorrimer at the poker table. But then the discussion shifted.

"I think we oughta play him on the rag," Singleton said. "It's the tightest game we got, and it's not all over the papers."

Hooker knew that "rag dealers" peddled phony stocks—either blue-sky shares in nonexistent corporations, or counterfeit certificates. Hooker couldn't believe anyone would fall for that kind of routine. But there had been a time he didn't believe they would pay twenty bucks for a phony diamond ring, either. If the setup was right, anything worked.

"Naw," Gondorff said. "I don't like the idea much of conning stocks to a banker."

"We gonna con the payoff to a gambler?" Singleton asked.

Gondorff thought for a while and then seemed to come to a decision.

"No," he said, "let's use the wire. Never known a gambler who wouldn't like to beat the ponies."

"Jesus, Henry," Niles said, "the wire's ten years outa date."

"Right. That's why he won't know it."

Singleton snorted. "I'm not sure *I* know it."

Gondorff was already figuring ahead. "We'll get on the train in Pittsburgh," he said, "and give him the hook in the poker game. Then we'll sting him here. You think I can get in that game, Eddie?"

"All you gotta do is show up with a roll of money and look like a fool."

"I also gotta win."

There was a light knock on the door. "It's me, Henry," Billie's voice said. Kid Twist unlocked the door.

She brought in a tray with five bottles of beer and put it on the table.

"You're looking lovelier than ever, Billie." Singleton smiled as she opened the bottles.

"Just good, clean living, J. J."

Billie squeezed between Gondorff and Hooker to serve the beer. When she was finished, she leaned close to Gondorff's ear.

"You know a dick named Snyder?"

Hooker looked sharply at her, then quickly dropped his eyes, casually reaching for a beer bottle.

"No," Gondorff said indifferently. "Should I?"

"He was just in here looking for a counterfeiter."

"Who?"

"I don't know. He didn't say his name. He said the guy hung around joyhouses."

Gondorff threw a quick glance at Hooker, but then seemed to discount the idea. "Okay," he said. "Let me know if you see him again.

"All right," Gondorff said when she left, "Singleton, me, Billie, and Hooker'll take the train to Pittsburgh tomorrow. By the time the train gets back into Chicago, we'll figure to have him hooked. So you guys'll have to work fast. I checked the other day, and Jenner's old pool hall is empty. Fix it up first class. We want it to look like the real thing. You know what I mean?"

Eddie Niles nodded.

"And get some clean people for boosts," Gondorff said to Twist, "guys who look like bankers and country clubs. And we'll need a legit wire from the telegraph office. Can you handle that, Eddie?"

"No problem," Niles said.

"Okay. I guess that's it."

"How much we goin' for?" Twist asked.

Gondorff smiled. "That depends how greedy Mr. Lorrimer is. The way I see it, he'd kill us just as dead for a buck as he would for a million. Whatd'ya think?"

Singleton shrugged. "I say all the way, Henry."

The others nodded.

"Okay." Gondorff smiled.

III. The Hook

Gondorff gave the cards a tight shuffle. He slid the two halves of the deck together, shuffled again, and smoothed the cards tightly into his right hand. He dealt one from the top, one from the bottom, and then held the top card and slipped out two from beneath it. He glanced questioningly at Billie.

Billie smiled and slowly shook her head. "How long's it been since you sharped?" She was sitting sideways in the train compartment, propped against pillows, a Hollywood fan magazine in her hand. She watched him deal four more cards, and returned to her magazine.

"It'll come back," Gondorff said. He stretched his fingers and flexed his knuckles and wrists. He glanced out the window and shuffled again. They were about halfway to Cleveland now, probably crossing from Indiana into Ohio. It all looked the same—broken-down depression farmhouses standing in barren, unplowed fields. The train clipped along toward Cleveland and Pittsburgh as if desperate to get back to the city.

"Whatd'ya think of the kid?" Gondorff asked.

"He's all right."

"He's damned good."

Billie gave him a skeptical glance. "He'd better be."

After they boarded the train, Gondorff had outlined the routine they were going to use on Lorrimer. Basically it was simple. Gondorff not only had to beat Lorrimer in the poker game; he had to infuriate him at the same time. Then Hooker would go to Lorrimer's compartment and give him his money back, pretending to double-cross Gondorff. The object was to get Lorrimer to trust Hooker. Once that was accomplished, and they were back in Chicago, Hooker could suck Lorrimer into the big play and the final sting.

Hooker's performance would not come until late, a little after the poker game. Hooker had asked a couple of questions, and then Singleton had taken him into the other stateroom to go over the details and drill him in his role. An hour later Hooker had come back for a test. Gondorff had played the part of Lorrimer and threw curves at the kid for half an hour. The questions covered everything from his childhood and schooling to his jobs, his friends and connections, and the who, what, where, and when of his activities in the past two weeks. Hooker had come through with flying colors, improvising his answers convincingly and without hesitation. Gondorff understood why Luther had been so high on him. He was sharp.

Gondorff practiced switching packets of five cards—poker hands—for a while. He palmed them, ostensibly scratched the back of his hand, and switched them to the other palm. He placed five cards facedown on the table, picked them up, and switched them with five others he had in his palm, placing the second five back on the table. Not too bad, he thought. He tossed them all on the table and stood up.

"I'm gonna get some air."

Billie grunted. "Bring some back for me."

He worked his way back through the swaying cars to the empty observation platform and leaned his elbows on the railing. He watched the tracks rush away from beneath him. The tension was starting to build.

Before a big play there was always a period in which he was convinced that every possible disaster was going to occur. It was natural. In the planning stages he always gave a great deal of thought to possible slip-ups. And those thoughts always seemed to accumulate and come back briefly to haunt him.

The first step of the play was up to Billie. He had no great fears about that. Her job was to lift Lorrimer's wallet. Assuming Lorrimer would come out of his compartment sometime before the poker game, she should be able to handle it. On a rocking train, there was no problem lurching into someone in the aisle.

As far as his own part was concerned, he was going into the poker game as if he were sloppy drunk. It was not an easy role to play. During the course of the game he'd have to drink heavily to make the performance convincing. But it was the fastest way to get Lorrimer's goat. He'd have to play it by ear, moving carefully once he got in there.

And Lorrimer would have a couple of his goons watching the game. Gondorff's card manipulations would have to be flawless.

And finally there was the question of Hooker. The kid was quick and seemed to be gutty. But practicing with Gondorff, and facing the real thing, with a couple of Lorrimer's heavies standing in the room, were two different things.

Hooker could probably handle it. But there was something else about the kid that bothered Gondorff. Before they had left Chicago, Eddie Niles had checked into the cop who dropped in at Billie's. He turned out to be a lieutenant on the bunco detail, and his territory was the same area Luther and Hooker used to work. It didn't seem likely they all hadn't bumped into each other two or three times. Gondorff wondered. Before they got too far along in the con, he might have to do something about that.

Gondorff took a deep breath and straightened from the rail. He let out the air with a rush, and smiled suddenly at his doubts and fears. They were a good sign. They meant he was still alert. The real trouble would come when he started a big play *without* a few stomach rumblings.

After they got off the train in Pittsburgh there was a forty-five-minute wait before the westbound train came through from New York. They had a cup of coffee and sat in the lobby watching the foot traffic.

"Getting nervous?" Gondorff asked Hooker.

"No," Hooker said. With his new suit and haircut he looked more like a young executive than an ex-street grifter. But from habit, Hooker's eyes scanned the people passing by, assessing them, picking out the most promising marks. The performance he was to give for Lorrimer didn't worry him too much. It was the remote possibility that Lorrimer or one of his goons might know who he really was, that would make this the shortest con in history.

"The important thing," Gondorff said, "is to forget Luther when you meet this guy. You don't ever wanta get emotionally tied up in this racket. He's just another mark, maybe a little smarter than the others. Just play it like you believe it, and you'll do okay."

"What if he doesn't buy it?"

Gondorff chuckled. "Then we go home and ride the merry-go-round."

The iron speaker announced the arrival of the New York train. It would be departing for Chicago in twelve minutes.

Their compartments were already reserved. For the return trip Hooker and Gondorff shared one and Billie and Singleton the other. They split up before they boarded. When the luggage was brought, Gondorff handed the porter a five and asked him to send the conductor around as soon as the train pulled out.

"Now," Gondorff said when the porter was gone, "you can just sit around for a while and look subservient."

"What's that mean?"

Gondorff laughed. He dug out a full bottle of bourbon from his suitcase and placed it prominently on the table. "It means you're a messenger boy. It means you jump when I say so. And you don't like it much."

Hooker smiled. "Okay. And my name is now Carver. Right?"

"That's the idea."

A light tapping sounded on the door. Gondorff smiled and picked up the bourbon bottle. He screwed off the cap and opened the door. It was the conductor.

"Porter said you wanted to see me, sir?"

"Yeah," Gondorff said. He swayed a little, giving the impression he'd had a few shots before he boarded, and motioned with the bourbon bottle. "C'mon in, c'mon in."

The man noted the bottle. He took a stiff step inside.

"Say," Gondorff said, and gave his nose a couple of pulls, "I had lunch with a guy who said there's a friendly poker game on this train. You know anything about that?"

"A little," the man said vaguely.

"You think you could get me in that game?"

The conductor glanced uneasily at Hooker. "I don't know," he said. "There's usually a waiting list."

Gondorff smiled. He opened his hand, showing a fifty-dollar bill. The conductor glanced at it and shrugged.

"That'll certainly get you first *alternate*, sir."

Gondorff flipped his thumb, turning over a second fifty.

The conductor's hand gathered in the money and slipped it smoothly into his pocket. "I'll see what I can do, sir."

"Yeah, you do that. Much obliged ... Carver!" Gondorff growled as the door was closing, "Get off your ass and get me some ice."

"Yes, sir," Hooker said promptly.

They both waited silently for a moment, until the conductor was gone. Gondorff smiled. "Now, you'd better get the porter to bring me some ice."

Singleton came in as Hooker went out. "You get in?" he asked Gondorff.

"Yeah, I think so. I gave the kayducer a C-note." He poured two inches of bourbon from the bottle into the sink. He poured another two inches into a water tumbler. He set the glass on the table and eased down in a seat. "How's Billie makin' out?"

"No show, so far. Lorrimer and his cronies are still in the dining car. You think she can handle him?"

Gondorff smiled. "Billie could lift your jock strap, and you wouldn't feel a thing. You find out the deck?"

"Yeah." Singleton tossed two sealed decks of cards on the table and sat down. "He usually plays with Royals or Cadenzas. I got one of each."

To beat Lorrimer at poker, he would have to beat him at cheating. And to beat him at cheating, he had to have the same brand of cards Lorrimer used. Gondorff peeled off the cellophane and fanned out the first deck. "What kind of stinger?"

"He likes to cold-deck low."

Gondorff smiled to himself. Lorrimer was fleecing amateurs, so he was trying to make it look legit by giving them handfuls of deuces or treys. At the same time, he dealt himself sevens or eights. Gondorff was tempted to use aces just to rub it in the bastard's face. He looked across the table at Singleton. "Whatd'ya think?"

"Jacks oughta be safe."

Gondorff thought a minute. "Yeah." He took four jacks and an ace from each of the decks and tossed the rest of the cards into his suitcase. He palmed the two sets of five cards and switched them three or four times.

"Not bad," Singleton said.

Hooker came back in with a bucket of ice. "I think Lorrimer's going back to his room. One of his goons just stationed himself at the end of the dining car."

"Billie see him?"

"Yeah, she's waiting in a seat by the aisle."

Gondorff took a deep breath. He smiled at each of them and slowly unwrapped a cigar. Hooker sat down, and all three gazed silently at nothing, waiting.

There were sounds of people passing outside the compartment. There was a muffled knock on the room next to them. They heard the porter say, "Thank you, sir," and the door closed. They waited.

Heavy footsteps sounded outside. There was a brushing against the door and the murmuring of deep voices. Then silence again.

They all looked up tensely as the door finally opened. Billie slipped quickly inside. She smiled, drew a thick alligator wallet from her coat pocket, and tossed it on the table. It was over.

"Any trouble?" Gondorff asked.

"Naw." Billie dug a cigarette out of her purse. "He didn't say a word. One of his gorillas grabbed me and pushed me away after I bumped him." She laughed. "I told him to get his dirty mitts off me or I'd call the conductor."

Gondorff lifted a bundle of money out of the wallet. He sorted through the bills and smiled, fanning them out. They were crisp new hundreds and five hundreds. "Fifteen grand," he said. "Looks like he was expecting a big night." He glanced over at Hooker. "You wanta quit now, kid?"

They all smiled.

An hour later the conductor came around and told Gondorff the game would begin in ten minutes. Gondorff checked his watch.

He waited for fifteen minutes, and got a clean shirt from his suitcase. He squeezed it into a tight ball several times, effectively wrinkling it, and put it on. He splashed bourbon on his face, sprinkled a little over his pants, and checked himself in the mirror. His hair was a little too neat. He mussed it on one side. Not bad, he thought. He looked like hell.

With Lorrimer's money in his pocket, he staggered a little into the next car. He made his way to the compartment number the conductor had given him and knocked heavily. The conductor opened the door. Gondorff moved past him, grinning broadly.

"Sorry I'm late, boys," he boomed. "I was taking a crap. When you gotta go, you gotta go, huh?" He stuck out a hand to no one in particular.

The rumpled hair and whiskey-sprinkled clothing had the desired effect. Including Lorrimer, there were four men seated at the poker table, all neatly dressed in suits and ties—a gathering of gentlemen. And the gentlemen were all appropriately startled by his crudeness.

No one made a move to shake the hand. On either side of the room two of Lorrimer's goons sat with their fists in their overcoat pockets, gazing impassively at him. The conductor stepped forward uncertainly.

"Mr. Shaw is a bookmaker from Chicago," he said a little tightly. "Mr. Shaw, meet Mr. Clayton from Pittsburgh, Mr. Jameson, Chicago, Mr. Lorrimer, New York, and Mr. Lombard from Philadelphia."

"Glada meecha," Gondorff responded to the circle of icy nods. "Guess this is my seat, huh?" He swayed a little and dropped into it. "Yes, sir"—he smiled—"nothing like a friendly poker game to pass the time."

The conductor placed two decks on the table. "Straight poker, gentlemen. One-hundred-dollar minimum, table stakes. It is assumed that all players are good for their debts." He placed three stacks of chips in front of Gondorff. "Three thousand dollars, Mr. Shaw."

Lorrimer was already shuffling the cards, his jaw tight as he watched them riffle through his fingers. He looked as cool and calculating as Gondorff expected. His hair was perfectly brushed, his mouth expressionless, and the eyes were two dull black disks. "Mr. Shaw," he said quietly, "we require a necktie at this table. If you don't have one, we can get one for you."

Gondorff looked surprised. "Yeah. Yeah, that'd be real nice, Mr. Lamnamer."

"The name is Lorrimer."

"Right," Gondorff said.

The conductor handed him a black tie. While Lorrimer dealt the first hand, he maneuvered it under his collar and then abandoned the task. He picked up his cards.

Straight poker is the simplest and most deadly form of the game. Five cards are dealt down. There are no draws, and the betting continues until all call or all but one drop out. It was going to be a long night, Gondorff decided.

"Say, how's chances of gettin' a bottle? Bourbon or gin's okay."

The porter got him a bottle.

Gondorff had once made a living at poker. That was a long time ago, during World War I, but he still remembered the labels he gave different players. There were the Rotarians—the players who were always anxious not to make any enemies, and never bluffed or raised too stiffly. It would embarrass them to win heavy. Clayton fit into this category. Jameson was the Math Professor. He knew all the odds, and statistically he could predict what every hand was likely to be. But how to make the most of it baffled him. Lombard was the Man from Peoria, where they never heard of poker. Lorrimer was the only real player. He pushed the good ones and bluffed pure dead man. Even without cheating, he could probably clean the three of them.

Gondorff played and drank and made bad jokes. Clayton smiled at some of them. Jameson and Lombard ignored them, and Lorrimer gritted his teeth. The chips were stacking up in front of Gondorff and Lorrimer, but the going was slow.

After three hours, Gondorff glanced at his watch and picked up the worst hand he had been dealt all evening. The highest card was an eight. It was time for action, he decided. He grinned and poured himself a healthy drink. "Open for a thousand."

"Raise five hundred," Lombard said.

Lorrimer stayed, and the other two dropped out.

"You gotta play 'em when you get 'em," Gondorff said. "Raise two thousand."

Lombard called, putting in twenty-five hundred. Lorrimer studied his cards.

Gondorff sighed. "Come on, Lorrihan. Jesus Christ, I never seen anybody think so goddamned much and then do the wrong thing. Bet 'em, or get out."

Lorrimer's eyes narrowed. He closed his hand. "See you, and raise a thousand."

Gondorff laughed and grabbed a handful of chips. "Now we're gettin' a little action around here. It's about time, for Christ's sake. I'll call your thousand and bump another two. Naw, shit. Make it three."

Lombard had about a thousand left in front of him. He could stay to the end by putting all of it in. He shook his head. "Too rich for me," he said, and tossed the cards away.

Lorrimer thought some more. He looked at his chips and back at his cards, then tossed them aside. "Out."

The pot was Gondorff's without showing his hand. A good poker player would quietly stick the cards back in the deck and let the other players try to guess if he'd been bluffing. Gondorff turned over the hand

and spread it out. "Jesus Christ, God a'mighty!" He laughed. "Lormaner, you're about the dumbest card player I ever ran across. Ya play with your head up your ass. Shit, if you can't beat an eight high, ya oughta go back to those penny-ante games in New York."

Lorrimer's teeth were grinding away at his fillings. Gondorff gave Lombard a pat on the back. "Tough luck, fella," he said.

Lombard smiled ruefully. "I'm afraid that's all for me."

"Aw, hell, don't feel bad about it, pal," Gondorff said. "Lemmoner over there wouldna even let ya in this game if you weren't a chump. Hell, you've been taken, buddy."

Lombard looked shocked, not so much by the suggestion that he had been cheated, but by Gondorff's appalling rudeness. Across the table, Lorrimer was boiling.

"What the hell do ya mean by that?" he demanded.

"What the hell do ya think I mean? Ya get these poor bastards in here every week and fleece 'em like babies."

Lorrimer's eyes blazed. He stood up suddenly. "I've had enough of your goddamned lip, Shaw!"

Gondorff looked up at him. "You're breakin' my fuckin' heart, Lassiter."

"You son-of-a-bitch!"

Gondorff rose slowly. He reached for the whiskey bottle, then quickly smashed it on the edge of the table, lifting the jagged end toward Lorrimer. "You just take it easy there, sonny boy. Nobody calls me a son-of-a-bitch."

Lorrimer's two thugs were up, one with a hand inside his coat. Both Jameson and Lombard had half-risen from their chairs, gaping, uncertain what to do.

"Let's all just take it easy, huh?" Jameson said thickly.

"Yes," Lombard said, and made an effort to smile.

"Why don't we all take a break for a couple of minutes and cool off?"

Gondorff waited, gazing steadily across the table. Lorrimer stared back at him, the muscles of his jaw working. "Okay," he said tightly, "five minutes."

He turned and strode past Gondorff and out the door. His two heavies glared and quickly followed.

In the compartment, Gondorff downed two cups of coffee and stretched out while Billie wiped his face with a wet towel.

"How long you figure?" Hooker asked.

"Ten, fifteen minutes," Gondorff said. Jesus, he thought, he'd conned a lot of people, but not when they were sitting around with guns.

By the look on Lorrimer's face when he left, he wasn't going to fool around. He was probably stacking a deck right now.

Gondorff took a couple of deep breaths and sat up. He slid the four jacks and the ace from his pocket and fitted them snugly into his palm. He turned the hand down and switched the cards to the other palm, then looked at Hooker and Billie. They both smiled.

All the players had returned. But only Jameson had bought a fresh stack of chips. The other two had moved their chairs back from the table, ready to kibbitz. The goons were back in position, and Lorrimer was waiting stiffly behind his chips, a look of cold determination on his face.

"Everybody cooled off?" Gondorff laughed. He dropped heavily into his chair and smiled. There was a fresh bourbon bottle at his elbow.

"Your deal, Mr. Shaw," Lorrimer said. He pushed the deck across the table.

Gondorff shuffled twice, keeping the cards flat on the table to avoid exposing his palmed cards. He slapped the deck on the table for Lorrimer to cut, and then deliberately took his eyes from it, struggling to open the whiskey bottle. "Glad to see you back in, Mr. Jameson," he said, and poured himself a large drink.

The cards were back in front of him. Lorrimer had worked smoothly. The braced deck had been substituted for the cards Gondorff had shuffled. Lorrimer's left hand was now disappearing casually under the table, disposing of the original deck.

Gondorff picked up the new deck and slapped it into his hand. He kept the five palmed cards separated from the others with his little finger, and dealt. "Feeling lucky, Mr. Lorriman?" he sneered as he tossed the cards out.

Lorrimer ignored the question.

Gondorff smiled. He cleared his throat noisily and picked up his hand, fitting it smoothly together with the palmed cards.

"Check," Jameson said.

Gondorff smiled to himself. It looked like Lorrimer wasn't interest in sucking Jameson into the pot. Apparently he had nothing. Gondorff held his cards close to the edge of the table and fanned out only the five he had dealt himself. He had four threes and a queen. He closed the cards and one by one he idly transferred the top five to the bottom while he gazed thoughtfully at Lorrimer.

"Bet five hundred," Lorrimer said.

Gondorff squinted down at his cards again, this time fanning out the four jacks and the ace. He closed the hand and placed it on the table, palming the other five cards. "Raise five hundred."

"Fold," Jameson said.

"Raise a thousand," Lorrimer said.

Gondorff picked up the whiskey bottle. He poured himself a large drink and looked very carefully across the table. Lorrimer was expressionless. The level gaze betrayed none of the confidence the man must be feeling. "Raise three thousand," Gondorff said.

Lorrimer counted chips and shoved them in. "Raise two thousand."

Lorrimer was playing it smart, keeping his raises smaller than Gondorff's. This was supposed to indicate he had less confidence in his hand than Gondorff did. Gondorff ponderously cut out seven piles of chips from the stack in front of him. "See your two, and raise five thousand."

The silent spectators all looked at Lorrimer now. Clayton reached forward and quietly snubbed out his cigarette. Lorrimer studied his hand again. He finally closed the cards. He set them to the side, smiled faintly, and with both hands pushed forward all the chips in front of him. "I'll see you, Shaw," he said, "and raise the rest."

Gondorff acted startled. He placed his forearm behind his chips and scraped them into the center of the table. "Call."

For the first time, Lorrimer smiled. Without looking down, he reached for his cards and turned them over in a neat little stack. One by one, he casually tapped them apart with his fingertip. "Four nines," he said. The smile broadened, and the lidded eyes gazed at Gondorff with cool, victorious contempt.

There was a faint whistle from Clayton, and even Lorrimer's goons allowed their mouths to show a little twist of pleasure.

Gondorff stared at the cards with amazement. Then he eased back in the chair a little and let out a sigh of relief. The feeling of relief was more genuine than he would have liked. The possibility that Lorrimer had stacked himself something better than jacks had begun to haunt him through the last couple of bets. He smiled and turned over the four jacks.

Clayton, Jameson, and Lombard were aghast, murmuring with astonishment over the appearance of two such powerful hands.

Lorrimer looked as if the floor had suddenly disappeared from under him. The smile was gone. The blood had drained from his face, and now it was all coming back with a rush. He looked at the cards, at Gondorff, back at the cards, and then glared furiously at one of his heavies—no doubt the man who had stacked the deck for him.

The goon's mouth hung open, his head slowly shaking with denial.

"Well, boys," Gondorff said, and began scraping in the chips, "that's all for me tonight. Like I said, there's nothing like a friendly poker game to pass the time on a train." He smiled. "I'll be glad to leave you a little cab fare if you need it."

The conductor glanced hesitantly at Lorrimer, then discreetly placed a sheet listing their debts in the middle of the table. All except Lorrimer drew out wallets and began counting bills.

Gondorff abruptly stopped pulling in chips and looked at Lorrimer. "You owe me fifteen grand, pal."

The two goons had moved forward a step, ready for action if they were signaled. Lorrimer was too confused and angry to notice them. He reached inside his coat.

Gondorff watched as the hand stiffened. Again the look of incredulity came to Lorrimer's face. The hand dug deeper into the pocket and came out. Both hands moved down to the side pockets, then to the rear. They found nothing.

Lorrimer looked at his goons, and then at Gondorff. A sick smile came to his face for an instant as he stood up. "I guess I left my wallet in my room."

"What?!" Gondorff exploded as Lorrimer started for the door. "Don't give me that crap, you little turd! How do I know you ain't gonna take a powder?" Gondorff pulled his own wallet from his pocket and thrust it out, spreading it to show the wad of bills. "You come to a game like this, you bring money, pal!"

"You son-of-a-bitch," Lorrimer said tightly. He moved toward Gondorff, but the conductor quickly stepped between them.

"Perhaps, if you will permit Mr. Lorrimer to go to his room..."

Gondorff grabbed the stack of bills the other men had put in front of him and stood up. "All right, buddy," he said, and shook the money at Lorrimer. "I'm gonna send a boy to your room in five minutes. And you'd better have that jack, friend, or it's gonna be known all over Chicago that your name ain't worth a dime." He wheeled, stormed out the door, and slammed it behind him.

In the corridor, Gondorff glanced in both directions. It was all clear. He moved rapidly toward the back of the train.

His hands were damp. His heart thumped with heavy, shuddering beats, and the alcohol was starting to play tricks with his vision. But he had made it. Old Henry S. Gondorff still had the touch.

He grinned and gave an okay signal to Singleton at the far end of the car and turned into the compartment.

Billie looked up anxiously from her solitaire game. Hooker sat up quickly in the seat. Gondorff shut the door behind him and sighed. "Well"—he grinned and dropped heavily in the seat—"we got ourselves a little workin' money." He tossed the wad of bills on the table.

"You think he's ready?" Hooker asked.

"He's ready." Gondorff put the fifteen thousand back in Lorrimer's wallet and gave it to Hooker. He dropped his head on a pillow and lifted his feet with a groan. "Just take it easy, kid."

He folded his hands over his chest and began to snore.

"Good luck, kid." Billie smiled. "Don't bother to call for help."

Outside the compartment, Hooker stood for a moment balancing himself against the swaying train.

"Be in Chicago in fifteen minutes, sir," a porter said, and hurried by.

Hooker moved toward Lorrimer's compartment. Relax, he told himself. What he had to do was simple. Just play it cool. His name was Johnny Carver. He worked for Henry Shaw, who ran a bookie joint in Chicago. He hated Shaw's guts. He wanted to get Shaw, and if Lorrimer was interested, they might work together and wipe out the fat son-of-a-bitch. Hooker smiled. His heart was clicking along a little faster than usual. But it felt good to be back in action again.

At Lorrimer's door, he stopped. He took a long breath and knocked.

"My name is Carver," he said when the door opened a crack. "Mr. Shaw sent me."

"It's Shaw's boy."

It was a double-sized compartment. Lorrimer was sitting in a chair, smoking, his tie loosened and one foot propped against a low table. He was smaller than Hooker had expected. But there was no flab on the chunky body. The two goons, with their black overcoats, were right out of the catalog.

Lorrimer took a long drag on the cigarette and blew the smoke out slowly. "Your boss is quite a card player, Carver. How does he do it?"

Lorrimer didn't seem to expect an answer. He was staring at his cigarette as if wondering why the hell he was smoking it.

"He cheats," Hooker said matter-of-factly.

Lorrimer squinted up at him, not particularly pleased with the answer. For a second the eyes flashed, but then he seemed to shrug it off. He pulled a checkbook from his coat and picked up a pen from the table. "He's gonna have to take a check. I couldn't find my wallet."

"Yeah," Hooker said. "He knows that."

The pen stopped in midair. Lorrimer looked up

again, this time not prepared to shrug it off. "Whatd'ya mean?"

Hooker pulled the wallet from his pocket and tossed it over. "He hired a dame to take it from ya."

Lorrimer caught the wallet. He glanced at the bills inside and tossed it on the table. Amon Lorrimer did not like surprises. He liked playing the part of a fool even less.

"You were set up, Lorrimer," Hooker said. "Shaw's been plannin' to beat your game for months. He was just waitin' for ya to cheat him so he could clip ya."

Lorrimer looked over at his henchmen and back to Hooker. "I could have you put under the train for this, errand boy."

"So could Shaw."

"Then why the rat?"

" 'Cause I'm tired of bein' his nigger. I want you to help me break him."

It was hard to tell what Lorrimer thought about that. For a full minute he gazed silently at Hooker, at the new suit and tie and the neatly barbered hair.

"Where'd ya get on the train, Carver?"

"Pittsburgh."

"You mean the three of ya came all the way from Pittsburgh just to bust me?"

"Naw, we had other business in Pittsburgh."

"What's your game, Carver?"

"Whatd'ya mean?"

"I mean you're a fuckin' liar. There's four of ya on this train. There's a red-faced guy with spats been hangin' around, an' he's got the same compartment as the dame. Ain't that right, Boyle?"

The goon by the door nodded.

Stay cool, Hooker told himself. "Yeah," he said, "that's Bartlett. He was already in Pitt settin' up a deal. He didn't come out with us."

"You're pretty quick, Carver."

Hooker nodded. When in doubt, take the offensive.

"Look," he said, "if you ain't interested, just gimme the check an' I'll find somebody else to help me."

Lorrimer gave him a contemptuous smile and wrote out the check. He stood up and handed it to Hooker, getting his topcoat as the brakes began to moan beneath them. "You're a smart kid, Carver, but you'd better watch your step."

"You wanta bust him, or don't ya?"

"I don't give a shit about Shaw."

"Okay," Hooker said. He turned for the door.

"You live in Chicago?" Lorrimer asked.

"Yeah."

"I'll give ya a ride home."

Hooker hesitated, glancing at the heavies.

"What'sa matter," Lorrimer sneered, "you gotta get back to Shaw?"

"Naw." Hooker shrugged. "He's passed out. Can't see him till morning anyway."

"All right, then," Lorrimer said.

"Okay. I'll get my bag."

Back in the compartment, Billie had hoisted Gondorff to a sitting position. She was slapping his face, trying to get a cup of coffee into him.

"Are we still alive?" she asked Hooker.

"I don't know." Hooker got his bag down from the rack and headed out.

"If you see J. J., tell him to get his ass in here," Billie said desperately. "And tell him to bring some salt."

Hooker smiled and left.

Lorrimer was waiting beside the train with one of the bodyguards. When he saw Hooker, he strode off through the station, and Hooker followed. A black limousine was waiting at the curb.

"Where ya live?" Lorrimer asked when they got in the back seat.

Hooker gave the address. The driver nodded, and they rode in silence. Hooker watched the streets through the first couple of turns and then relaxed. They appeared to be headed for his apartment.

Lorrimer finally lit a cigarette and stared out a side window. "What're ya gonna tell Shaw when he asks for the fifteen grand from my wallet?"

Hooker shrugged. "I keep his books. I'll tell him I put it in the bank."

Lorrimer finally looked over at him. "Okay, so you wanta get Shaw. Why come to me?"

"I need somebody respectable. But not completely legit. What I'm gonna do ain't legal."

"I'm a banker, friend. In this state, that's legit."

Hooker nodded. "All you gotta do is place a bet for me at Shaw's place. I'll supply all the money and the information."

"A bet on a horse?"

"Right."

"This Shaw's really a bookie, huh? I never heard of him."

"That's the way he likes it. Strictly a quiet, red-carpet operation. All high rollers." Hooker pulled Lorrimer's check from his pocket. "If ya help me out, I'll pay off the money you owe Shaw myself." He tore up the check and held out the pieces.

"It's worth fifteen grand to ya?"

"A lot more than that. Maybe a couple of million."

Lorrimer glanced at the torn check. He looked at Hooker and out the window again. The mention of a couple of million apparently had stirred some interest.

The car slowed, eased quietly over to the curb, and Hooker got out. He held the door open while the driver got his bag from the back. "If you're interested," he said, "be at 660 Marshall Street at twelve-thirty tomorrow."

"That where Shaw's place is?"

"It's around the corner from there."

Lorrimer nodded faintly, suddenly looking bored by the whole thing. "I'll think about it, kid. But don't count on me. If I'm not there by a quarter of one, I'm not coming."

Hooker stood for a moment, thinking, feeling the damp, early-morning chill on his face. He wasn't sure about Lorrimer. The guy seemed more interested in the location of Gondorff's bookie joint than in placing the bet.

Well, to hell with it, Hooker thought. He was hungry. He took his bag up to his room and then went out the fire door to the alley.

There was an all-night diner over on Archer. And there were usually cabs waiting out front. In case they got separated, Gondorff had said to meet him at Jenner's old pool hall. Hooker smiled, wondering if Gondorff would be in any condition to talk.

Once out of the alley, he jammed his hands in his pockets and headed west. He wondered what Luther would have thought of his performance. He'd have given Hooker a little advice to dampen his cockiness. The play isn't over, he would say, not until you've got the money and you've made it around the corner. And you're not home free until you're sure someone like Snyder isn't waiting in the alley for you.

Snyder. Hooker had forgotten about him in the last twenty-four hours. But Snyder wouldn't be up at this time of night. By now the bastard would have counted his shakedown money, stuffed it into his coffee can and gone happily to bed.

At Archer, Hooker angled across the dark street and headed for the red neon sign that said "EAT" at the far corner. There was a cab in front of the restaurant, the driver dozing with his head against the side window.

Hooker looked into the diner. He saw a bum curled over a cup of coffee, and the two men at the rear of the counter wearing fedoras and overcoats. He had pushed open the door and moved a step inside before the bell inside him issued its warning. For an instant Hooker froze, a burst of adrenalin gushing into his veins. There was no question about the two men. As quickly as the door opened, they both turned and looked. Riley and Cole. And for a split-second they were as startled as Hooker was.

In the next instant Hooker was gone. He dived into the back of the cab, at the same time shaking the driver's shoulder. "Get the hell out of here!" he yelled. "Fast!"

The two men were moving toward the front door of the diner. The one in the lead had already pulled a gun. Hooker dropped to the floor.

The back tires of the cab squealed. Hooker was thrown against the side door as they whipped sharply around a corner.

"What the hell's going on?" the cabby asked.

Hooker rose in the seat again. He peered out the back window. The two men were climbing into a parked car.

"Turn right, quick!"

The driver slowed down and wheeled into a narrow street. There was barely space to pass between the parked cars, and he drove cautiously.

"Take a right at the corner," Hooker said.

"Hey, what's the story, Mac?"

Hooker watched out the window. A pair of headlights swerved into the narrow street just as the cab turned out. "Speed it up, can't ya?" Hooker said. Riley and Cole wouldn't be so cautious about the parked cars.

The cabby gave it a little more throttle. "Hey, look," he said, "I don't want no trouble. Are those guys after you or something? I only been on this job two weeks." He was glancing nervously from the mirror to the street, as if counting the number of his dependents who would shortly be destitute.

"All right," Hooker said, "take me to the docks. It's only a couple of minutes."

"What good is that gonna do ya?"

"I got friends there. Just drive and shut your yap."

Hooker thought about Angie's Diner. He had no idea if anybody there could help him. It probably wasn't even open at this time of night. But no other ideas came to him. He sure as hell couldn't go to Gondorff.

The man whipped through another sharp right and speeded up. Behind them, Riley and Cole made the same turn within two seconds. They were gaining.

Jesus, Hooker thought. What the hell was he going to do? If only the cabby could give him a decent lead before they got to the docks. "Come on," he said, and looked back. Riley and Cole were a block and a half behind now, and the cabby was giving it all he had.

"At the waterfront, turn left and let me off a block after that."

The cabby nodded. He glanced in the mirror and clenched his teeth as the tires screeched through a broad left turn. He gave it one more spurt of gas, holding it for half a block, then hit the brakes.

Hooker held the door open. As quickly as the car came to a stop he leaped out and barreled full speed toward Angie's. He heard the taxi speed away behind him. Then he came to a skidding halt in front of the diner. It was closed. Only a small night light burned behind the counter.

Hooker pounded hopelessly on the door, knowing there was no chance of anyone opening it in time to help him. He looked back at the sound of squealing tires, and ran again, ducking between the diner and a marine-equipment store, heading for the docks beyond.

He hesitated when he reached the open space. The dock ran for a quarter of a mile along the waterfront. A huge fenced warehouse ran along one side. On the other side was a thirty-foot drop into the water. Dim floodlights illuminated the area. A freighter was moored a hundred yards down. But it was dark, with no sign of a gangplank. His only chance would be to find one of the warehouse gates open. Hooker ran. Behind him he could hear Riley and Cole shouting to each other. They were probably separating, one coming up from behind and the other circling the warehouse to cut him off.

Hooker reached the first gate and yanked on the clasp. It was locked. Behind him he saw one of the men rounding the corner at the back of the diner. It was too late to make a break across the open dock toward the water. He looked the other way. Near the freighter there were a couple of dozen stacks of cargo crates. It was his only chance now.

Hooker ran blindly through the shadows. He passed fork trucks and winches and scrap bins, miraculously tripping over none of them. Almost there, he heard a voice behind him shout, "There he is!" Then he was in the midst of the crates, panting heavily, looking around desperately for a hiding place. He glanced up. There was no way to climb to the top; the sides were too smooth. He moved deeper into the stacks, then jumped quickly to the side as he saw a shadow come into view thirty feet ahead of him.

A shot suddenly broke the stillness. There was the simultaneous thud and splintering of wood in the crate to Hooker's right. He gasped for breath, looking off into the shadows on his left.

"Cole?" a voice yelled. "Move over to the other side. He just ducked in that next aisle."

Hooker moved past two aisles and two more stacks of crates. It was a losing game. There was only one more row of crates between him and the fence, and they were closing in on him. He stood perfectly still, listening. Then he looked down at the tangle of canvas at his feet. It was a long shot, but it might work.

"Okay," a voice shouted, "now move in another row."

Hooker had his coat off. He quickly bunched up the canvas to the size of a crouching man and fitted his coat around it. He dropped to his hands and knees and positioned the mound so it was partially visible along the aisle next to the fence. He stood up and flattened himself against the crates.

"Okay," a voice said, "Move in one more."

Hooker held his breath and looked off toward the waterfront. There was a clear lane between the crates and out across the dock to the water. He closed his eyes and waited.

There was the sharp crack of a pistol. Hooker opened his eyes. Another shot quickly sounded.

"He's back here," a voice shouted. "Right by the fence!" Three more shots came in quick succession.

Hooker waited two more seconds, long enough for the other man to move back to the fence. Then he turned and bolted toward the water. He was past the crates and into the open. Ten more strides, he told himself. The firing behind him was almost continuous now, and then he was suddenly off the dock. There was nothing beneath him, he was flying through the air, his arms outspread, plummeting downward, his legs groping blindly at nothing.

"Hooker show up yet?"

"Not yet," Twist said.

Gondorff looked at his watch. It was a quarter to five. The train had pulled into the station a little after two. Gondorff wondered. But Lorrimer might have taken him to breakfast. Or up to his hotel to question him. That was assuming Hooker hadn't slipped up on anything. Gondorff nodded and looked around.

The work was almost completed. They were still unloading a truck outside, bringing in more tables and chairs and sections of a bar. But the floor was all carpeted. The phones and cages and blackboards and ticker gear, along with a fancy chandelier, had been installed. Jenner's old pool hall was well on its way to becoming a posh, exclusive bookie joint. It looked good.

"Where'd you get the stuff?"

"Benny Garfield," Twist said. "He stuck us an extra

grand for the bar and the fancy counter, but I figured it was worth it."

"Yeah," Gondorff agreed, "we gotta go first class with this guy. How about the lookout?"

"We got a room across the alley. Got a good view of the entrance. And Phelan rigged us a buzzer."

"Good." Gondorff moved behind the counter, where Eddie Niles was making up boodles of fake bankrolls, bundling green paper with real hundred-dollar bills on the tops and bottoms. Gondorff watched and then sat down at a newly arrived table.

He was tired. Before they left the train, Billie had forced salt water into him until he vomited most of the alcohol. Then he had stuffed himself with solid food in the coffee shop at the station. But the hours were catching up with him.

"Okay," he said. "Who've you lined up to boost?"

Twist sat down across the table. "I got twenty, like you said. I figure I'll be handling the buzzer across the alley. Hooker, of course, will be the doorman and flunky. You and Eddie behind the cashier's cage, and J. J. will do the race-calling in the back room. Here's a list of the others."

Gondorff looked at the list. He smiled at the first name and looked up. "Curly Jackson? That the guy that does the English accent?"

"Yeah."

Gondorff nodded. A phony English aristocrat would be impressive to a man like Lorrimer. Gondorff had worked with four or five of the other men on the list. They were good, all experienced in some kind of con. He had heard of most of the others. "Boudreau help you?"

Twist nodded. "He's a little worried about your being federal, though. He says if this thing blows up, he can't do us any good downtown."

Gondorff grunted softly. He had hoped the Florida thing had been forgotten by now. Apparently the senator was still burning, still firing his famous memos to the FBI.

"I told him not to worry about it," Twist said.

Gondorff looked up as Eddie Niles banged a stack of bills on the counter, smoothing them out. Eddie was squinting across at the door. "Well," he said dully, "look who's here."

Gondorff looked around, suddenly relieved by the figure of Johnny Hooker coming through the door. Hooker had changed his clothes. He was wearing a heavy black sweater and the dirty pants Gondorff had seen the first day they met.

Hooker stopped in the middle of the outer room and looked around, impressed. "You know anywhere a guy can place a bet?"

"Million-dollar minimum," Niles said. He banged another stack of bills and banded them. Hooker moved past the counter and sat down, still admiring the surroundings.

Everything had worked out okay, Gondorff decided.

"Everything go all right?"

"Yeah. It was easy." Hooker smiled. He looked over at Eddie Niles, fascinated by the preparations.

"You see anything tonight?" Gondorff asked.

Hooker turned back. "Whatd'ya mean?"

"Like somebody tailin' you? A torpedo or something?"

Hooker looked surprised. "No, not a thing."

Gondorff relaxed, dismissing the suspicions. They were both tied up; Hooker was probably still high over his first success, and Gondorff was desperately in need of sleep. "Okay." He smiled, "How about Lorrimer?"

"I gave him the breakdown, just like you told me."

"And?"

"He threatened to kill me."

Gondorff laughed. "Hell, they don't do *that,* and you

know you're not getting through to 'em. Then what happened?"

"He drove me home. That's why I'm late. He tried to put himself away as legit. So I went right into the pitch."

"Did he hold you up on anything?"

"Naw. He just sat there and listened."

It sounded good. Very good. "That's fine," Gondorff said. "Once they start listening they're in trouble."

"You think he'll show?"

"Did he say he wouldn't?"

"No."

Gondorff smiled. "He'll show."

IV. The Tale

Hooker ordered his third cup of coffee. The waitress, a sixty-year-old woman who was probably the druggist's wife, delivered it to the booth. She slopped most of it into the saucer.

"Is that the right time?" Hooker asked. A big clock was hanging crookedly on the dusty wall over the soda fountain. It said twelve-fifty-two.

"Always has been," the woman said. She worked over the bill, changing the ten to fifteen cents, and ambled wearily back toward the kitchen.

Hooker was wearing a tuxedo, his uniform for the day. Rather than going back to his apartment, he had slept in the "store," stretched out on the carpet in front of the bar. It was a waste of time, he told Gondorff, to go home and then come back four hours later.

At ten-thirty, Singleton had come in and woke him up. He had a bag of doughnuts, and he made coffee on the hotplate. Ten minutes later Billie and Gondorff showed up. Then the others began filing in. By eleven the place was packed. Some of them came already dressed. Others, including Hooker, changed in the back room. From a seedy bunch of grifters they were suddenly transformed into a classy-looking group of gamblers.

When they were all dressed, Gondorff had a rehearsal. He placed people around the outer room, some at tables, others standing, and coached them on their movements and conversation. Racing forms were distributed. A man with headphones chalked names of horses, along with their odds, on the sliding blackboard panels. Behind a partition another man worked a phony switchboard, ringing the six phones behind the counter, while two men scurried to answer them, scribbling down numbers, pretending to take large bets.

The rehearsal looked good. Gondorff made a few changes, and at noon they broke for sandwiches and coffee. The paper cups and plates were cleaned up, and at twelve-twenty-five everyone took his place, ready. Hooker went out the alley door and crossed the street to the drugstore.

He sat in a booth near the back, directly across from the wall telephone, and ordered coffee.

It was an old drugstore. Along with the surrounding neighborhood, it had seen better days. Hooker waited, looking idly across the dusty displays of cosmetics, stationery and greeting cards, and past the reversed lettering that said "DRUGS—PRESCRIPTIONS" on the front window.

After fifteen minutes he ordered a second coffee. Two bums came in and sat at a front booth. But there was no sign of Lorrimer. Hooker wondered if he might have called or sent a message to his apartment house sometime during the morning.

An even darker thought hovered in his mind. It was possible Lorrimer had found out who he really was. He had probably talked to Riley and Cole this morning. They could have compared notes and come up wih the right answer. Hooker's stomach twisted a little when he considered these possibilities. But he deliberately pushed them from his mind. He finished off his cold coffee and ordered another.

Now, with the third cup in front of him, he looked up at the clock again. Twelve-fifty-six. Lorrimer said if he wasn't there by twelve-forty-five he wasn't coming. It didn't look good. He dumped two teaspoons of sugar in the coffee and filled it to the top with cream.

The bell had jingled, and two men were coming in. Neither of them was Lorrimer. But they could be a couple of his goons. They had that look—the dull black eyes and expressionless faces. They stood by the door for a moment, one of them looking over the two bums in the front booth. The other's eyes drifted slowly around and finally stopped on Hooker.

Hooker pushed the coffee to the center of the table and waited, his throat dry. If they were after him, there was no chance of escaping now.

They slid into the booth next to Hooker's, facing him, and then sat silently. The one closest to the aisle lifted his hand and made a quick gesture, waving the waitress off.

"Carver?"

The voice came from behind him. He stiffened, then turned quickly. Lorrimer was sitting in the booth directly in back of him, grinning smugly. In the booth behind him was the bodyguard who had gotten off the train.

"You should always look to the back too, kid," Lorrimer said.

Hooker smiled weakly. He left his coffee and slid quickly into Lorrimer's booth. "I was afraid you weren't coming. We haven't got much time."

Lorrimer shrugged indifferently. "Okay, get on with it, then."

Hooker nodded toward the telephone. "Sometime after one o'clock a guy's gonna call here and give you the name of a horse." He pulled a roll of bills from his pocket. "All you gotta do is take this two grand across the street to Shaw's place and bet it on that pony. There's nothing to it. But don't take too much time. We only got three or four minutes after you get the call."

Lorrimer snorted softly. "You figurin' to break him with a two-thousand dollar bet?" He lifted the money and tossed it back.

"This is just a test," Hooker said. "The big one comes later. Be careful with that, though." He pushed the money back. "It's all the money I got."

Lorrimer looked scornfully at the stack of bills and then at Hooker. "With that kind of dough, you were going to pay off Shaw for me?"

"I am after this race."

"You think you're gonna get rich on the ponies, huh?"

"Just do it, will ya? The place is right across the street about a hundred feet down the alley. And I gotta get back before Shaw misses me."

Lorrimer watched him get up, with mild distaste, as if he expected something more interesting for his time.

"Will ya do it?" Hooker asked desperately.

Lorrimer looked at the money. He picked it up slowly and nodded. "Yeah, I'll do it."

"Okay. Good luck," he said, and hurried for the door.

Outside, as he crossed the street, he glanced up at the second-story window above the alley. He could see Kid Twist watching from behind the curtain. Hooker gave him the "office," brushing his hand across his nose, and continued down the alley to the store.

When he walked in, the place was deathly silent, all eyes questioning him. Hooker smiled. "He showed."

"We'll let him stew a while," Gondorff said, leaning against the counter. "Tell Twist to call him the first winner he gets at big odds."

They waited. The girls emptied ashtrays and replaced stale drinks with fresh ones. Twist kept his eye on the ticket machine they had set up in his room. Garfield had gotten it for them for half a grand. Race results were coming in from all over the country, but so far Twist hadn't seen a winner at better than five to two.

Then, at 1:40 Twist got his horse. An eight to one shot named Bluenote had stumbled home first in the second race at Belmont Park. Immediately he dialed the number at the drugstore. All Lorrimer heard when he answered was, "second race. Belmont. Bluenote at eight to one, on the nose." Twist repeated it once and hung up.

Again they waited. Then the buzzer sounded, indicating the call had been made and that Lorrimer and his men were coming out of the drugstore.

"Okay," Gondorff said.

The place sprang into life. Suddenly people were moving around, talking to each other. Telephones rang behind the counter. Two men hurriedly answered them, ostensibly repeating large bets as they noted them on pads. The boardman moved along erasing and putting up new odds on horses. The girls moved briskly through the noisy crowd, bringing fresh drinks to the tables.

Two minutes passed before the knock came on the door. Hooker opened it a crack. It was one of Lorrimer's bodyguards. Hooker let him in.

No one looked at the man. He stood just inside the door for half a minute, watching the activity, giving people a quick once-over. Then he turned and leaned out the door.

Lorrimer came in with the two other bodyguards. He too gave the place a quick once-over. Then the three heavies fanned out into the crowd, and Lorrimer moved toward the betting window. He took his place in line behind two other men. The first one, Curly Jackson, plunked down two bundles of bills.

"Fifty thousand on War Eagle," he said.

Eddie Niles scribbled the figure and looked up. "Would that be to win, Mr. Bruce?"

"Yes, yes, quite," Jackson said. "On the nose, as they say."

Niles pushed the money aside. He gave Jackson his slip and looked up as the next man came forward. Behind him, Gondorff moved busily up to the counter. He spotted Lorrimer and snorted contemptuously.

"Never get enough, huh, pal? I'd think you'd get tired of losin', Horriman."

"The name is Lorrimer."

"Make sure you get cash from that guy, Eddie. He's got the name for bettin' money he don't have."

Lorrimer barely managed to supress his anger as Gondorff turned and walked away.

The next customer was still studying his racing form as he moved up. "Ummm, let's see," he said, "thirty-five thousand on, ummm ... Dancing Cloud, I think. To win."

"Fine, sir." Niles scribbled out the slip. The man reached for his wallet, but Niles shoved the slip across the counter. "Your credit's always good here, Mr. Herschorn."

"Oh. Thank you so much," the man said, and turned away.

Lorriman stepped up and tossed the money down as if anxious to get it over with as quickly as possible. "Two thousand on Bluenote to win," he muttered.

Niles frowned at him. "Is that all?"

"Yes," Lorrimer said, "that's all."

As quickly as Lorrimer turned from the counter Gondorff nodded to J. J. Singleton in the closed booth at the back of the room.

Singleton switched on his microphone.

"Good afternoon, ladies and gentlemen," he said, "this is Arnold Rowe, your track caller for the second race at Belmont Park in New York. A mile and an eighth claiming race for four-year-olds and up. The horses are in the gate." He paused, then charged his voice with excitement: "And they're off! Out of the gate and down the stretch the first time, it's War Eagle first by a length, Jail Bait second by one and a half, Dancing Cloud third, followed by Lucky Lady, Mojo, Wit's End, Cycle Boy, and Bluenote trailing."

Lorrimer moved to the bar and ordered a bourbon and soda. He looked over the crowd as the bartender made the drink. The place was quiet now, everyone listening to the call of the race. The girls moved around wiping tables and cleaning ashtrays.

The horses went into the clubhouse turn with Bluenote still bringing up the rear, eight lengths behind the leader. Lorrimer took his drink to an empty table and sat down. Some of the bettors were beginning to urge their horses on, their faces tense.

Lorrimer sipped his drink and glanced up dully as Hooker came to the table, gathering dirty glasses. "You really picked a loser, kid."

Hooker smiled confidently, keeping his voice low. "Give him a little time."

'Down the backstretch," the speaker crackled, "it's War Eagle holding on by a length, Dancing Cloud closing on the inside by two, Lucky Lady by one and a half, followed by Bluenote, Jail Bait, Wit's End, and Mojo."

"Come on, Dancing Cloud!" someone shouted, and a scattering of urgent yells erupted from the crowd.

Bluenote seemed to be moving up. There was a chance, Lorrimer supposed. He glanced off at one of his bodyguards in the corner. The man looked back and shrugged.

"Turning into the stretch," the announcer said, his voice rising, "it's Dancing Cloud by a length, War Eagle, and Bluenote making a move on the outside. Bluenote is now second and challenging the leader!"

Lorrimer finished off the drink. Around him the room had turned into a madhouse. People were screaming and banging folded racing forms on the tables, the announcer's voice hardly audible over the noise.

"Dancing Cloud and Bluenote. . . . Bluenote and Dancing Cloud; they're coming down to the wire and ... Bluenote wins it by a nose!"

A chorus of groans came from the bettors. They were all dropping back into their chairs, muttering, some of them swearing.

"Time for the mile and one eighth," the announcer said quietly, "is one minute forty-nine and four-fifths."

"Bloody awful!" Curly Jackson muttered at the table next to Lorrimer's. He tore up his betting slip and threw it in an ashtray. "Who in blazes is Bluenote?"

Lorrimer looked over at Hooker. The kid gave him a wink. Lorrimer smiled faintly and got up.

He casually tossed his slip to Eddie Niles and looked at Gondorff standing behind the counter. Gondorff was grim-faced. He watched Niles count out sixteen thousand dollars and push it across.

"Don't bother to come back with a piker's bet like that again, Lorrimer," Gondorff said. "We got a five-thousand-dollar minimum here." He looked past Lorrimer to Hooker. "Carver," he said, "show this man out."

Hooker looked startled, uncertain what to do.

"Go on," Gondorff shouted, "get him out of here!"

Lorrimer was already moving, ignoring the insults. His three heavies were waiting for him, holding the door open. Hooker shuffled along behind. After the four men strode out, he closed the door.

There was complete silence for a moment, everyone waiting to be certain Lorrimer was on his way. Then the buzzer sounded twice, Kid Twist's signal of all-clear.

A sigh of relief came from the crowd. They dropped into chairs, and Curly Jackson peeled off his Van Dyke beard, hurriedly scratching his itching chin. Gondorff smiled at Hooker.

"I think he's gaffed, kid."

Driving down to the cannery, Amon Lorrimer thought about Shaw's bookie setup and the Carver kid for a while, and then dismissed them from his mind. He had other more immediate problems.

From his hotel he had gone directly to the drugstore where he met Carver. But before he left, Al Coombs had called from the cannery. Riley was in the office. Last night he and Cole had found the kid who lifted the eleven thousand from Mottola. They had chased him down to the waterfront, Coombs told him, "But Riley thinks he got away."

"What the hell do you mean he *thinks* he got away?" Lorrimer had exploded. He told Coombs to keep Riley in the office until he got there, and then slammed the phone down.

Joe Leonard's idea to expand the organization in New York had appealed to Lorrimer. He had thought about it on the train and considered the possibilities of raising enough cash to get the ball rolling. But if his torpedoes couldn't even hit a small-time grifter, what the hell would happen when they had to battle people like Cappalo, or Luciano, or Dutch Schultz? And if the word got out that his muscle men were tripping all over themselves trying to make a patsy hit, his operations would get laughed off the street.

It was his own fault, Lorrimer told himself. Rolling heads was part of the game. And if every man in the organization, from the chiefs down to the runners, wasn't scared shitless for his life, they slacked off. He wondered about Al Coombs. Maybe he was the weak link in the chain. Ten years ago Coombs had been his top torpedo in New York. Lorrimer had sent him to Chicago because Coombs wasn't afraid to run liquor in competition with Capone. Coombs had done all right then. He had punctured enough of the O'Banion gang that Capone let him alone. But for the past five years Coombs had been sitting on his ass getting fat. And he had third-raters like Riley and Cole giving the whole outfit a bad image.

Coombs and Riley sat bolt upright as the door banged open and Lorrimer came in with the two bodyguards.

"Who's that?" Lorrimer demanded. A young kid was gaping at them from the chair next to Riley's.

"Greer," Coombs said, "you'd better wait outside."

The kid named Greer got shakily to his feet and moved around the wall behind the chairs toward the door.

Lorrimer waited until the door closed and turned abruptly to Riley. "What the hell happened?"

Riley was bent forward, his eyes on the floor. "We missed him."

"You missed him!" Lorrimer sneered. "That's not what I'm payin' you for."

Riley nodded. He gave Lorrimer a pained look. "It was dark out there. We didn't expect him to be so cagey. Besides, Cole screwed it up. He was supposed to cover the dock while I was firing."

"Where's Cole?"

"I dunno. He took off, I guess."

Lorrimer tossed his head toward the door. "Get out."

Riley stood up hesitantly. "The kid ran right by him. I was—"

"Get out!"

Riley glanced at the two stony-faced bodyguards. He smiled weakly, then slipped quickly past Lorrimer and out the door.

"What the fuck are you running here, Coombs?" Lorrimer asked. "Garule leaves that black bastard layin' out in the open, and now you got two knotheads shooting up the whole waterfront trying to hit a five and dime grifter."

Coombs nodded, avoiding Lorriner's eyes. He wiped his fingers across his forehead.

Lorrimer stared at him for a minute and then walked to the window. "Put Salino on it."

Coombs looked up with surprise. "Salino's the best

we got. This is just a small-time grifter we're dealin' with, Amon."

"Then why ain't he dead?"

Coombs chose to ignore the question. "Salino comes high," he said. "I think we could—"

"We'll use Salino," Lorrimer repeated. The matter was closed.

"How about Riley and Cole?"

Lorrimer looked at him. "What about 'em? Your hotshot, Cole, hasn't even come back."

"Yeah," Coombs conceded, "I doubt if we'll see him again unless he knows he's got a second chance."

"He's got a second chance, if he gets the job done before Salino does." Lorrimer smiled coldly. "Assuming he lives that long."

"Whatd'ya mean?"

"Salino don't like competition much."

Lorrimer was right. Salino would kill Cole on sight just to be sure Cole didn't get the credit for the killing. It was too bad. Cole was a good man. "You going back to New York tonight?" Coombs asked.

"I don't know. I may have some other business. You know a bookie named Shaw?"

"No."

"See what you can find out about him." Lorrimer gazed thoughtfully at him for a minute, then headed for the door.

"How about Riley?" Coombs asked.

Lorrimer stopped. Every time Coombs opened his mouth lately, it sounded like he was running a rest home for nearsighted gunmen. "Send him away for a little rest. It was bad enough he blew the hit. He shouldn'ta tried to blame it on Cole."

Coombs shrugged apologetically. "I'm sorry, Amon. I didn't know you wanted this grifter so bad."

"I didn't, till now," Lorrimer said. "You know his name?"

"Yeah. It's Hooker. Johnny Hooker."

Driving to the Sherman Hotel, the taxi took Hooker past the police station before it turned south on Michigan Avenue. Hooker paid no attention to the route they were taking. His thoughts were on Amon Lorrimer. The next part of the con was to sink the hook deeper, to convince Lorrimer that the race handicapping system was infallible, and still not appear too eager for his help.

There had been a message waiting for Hooker when he returned to his apartment. It was from Lorrimer, telling him to be at the Sherman at eleven in the morning. Hooker dropped in bed and slept for twelve hours. He phoned Gondorff first thing in the morning.

"As soon as you leave the hotel," Gondorff told him, "call Twist at the store. Figure at least two or three hours for Twist to set up the Telegram."

"Okay," Hooker agreed.

"Everything all right?" Gondorff asked. "Nobody following you, or hanging around your apartment?"

Hooker told him no. It was the third time Gondorff had asked him the same question.

The taxi left him at the curb, and Hooker strode confidently through the front door of the Sherman. Three steps inside, one of Lorrimer's heavies intercepted him.

"Nice day." Hooker smiled as they went up. The man stared straight ahead.

Hooker followed him down the hall on the fourth floor. The man unlocked a door and led him through a foyer and into a large sitting room.

Lorrimer was counting money behind a white desk, wearing a wine-colored smoking jacket. The two bodyguards sat in chairs on either side of the room, giving Hooker the usual stone-faced welcome. Hooker smiled broadly as he came in. "Well," he said, "what did I tell ya?"

Lorrimer placed a bundle of money to the side. He picked up another one and continued counting. "You're a lucky man, all right."

"Lucky, hell. I could do it every day."

"Why don't ya, then?"

"'Cause it's better to do it all at once. We're puttin' down seven hundred and fifty grand next week. At four to one, we make three million. If ya wanta stick with us, twenty percent of that is yours."

Lorrimer tossed the money on the desk and sat back. "What's your system, Carver?"

"You in?"

"Maybe."

Hooker pulled a chair close to the desk and leaned forward. "It's foolproof," he said. "We got a partner downtown runs the central office of the Western Union. Race results from all over the country come in there and go right across his desk on their way to the bookies." He let that sink in. "All he does is hold them up a couple of minutes until he can call us and we get a bet down on the winner. Then he releases the results to the bookies, and we clean up on a race that's already been run. It can't miss."

Lorrimer put an elbow on the chair arm and gently rubbed his chin. "Not bad," he said. He came forward, pushed a stack of bills across the desk, and sat back again. "You got the seven hundred and fifty grand yet?"

Hooker smiled. He picked up the money and thumbed through it. "Not yet, but . . ." He suddenly frowned at the money. "Hey, there's only two grand here!"

Lorrimer ignored the statement. "I think we oughta place another bet tomorrow."

"Come on, what is this?" Hooker said angrily. "That sixteen grand was my money. You tryin' to muscle me?"

"If your system is as foolproof as you say," Lorrimer said quietly, "you'll get even more."

"I'll decide when we lay the bets."

"Not if you want me to keep makin' them for you."

Lorrimer was smiling easily, figuring he'd backed

Hooker into a one-way street, and there was nothing the dumb kid could do about it. Hooker shoved the money inside his coat pocket. "I'll have to talk to my partner. We can't afford to expose our game too much."

"Let me talk to him."

"No," Hooker said emphatically.

"You want your money back? Try to get it in a court of law." Hooker was beat, and Lorrimer knew it. "C'mon, kid," he said with a laugh, "don't be a sorehead. I'll make it worth your while. Might even help ya finance the big play if the next one works out."

Hooker fidgeted a little, wrestling. "Yeah," he finally said, "Okay."

Lieutenant Ray Snyder tossed aside the frayed copy of *Liberty* magazine and looked up at the wall clock behind Captain Christiansen's secretary. It was twenty minutes to ten.

"It'll be about five minutes," the girl had said when Snyder first came in. That was twenty minutes ago. The girl had gone off for a cup of coffee and come back and typed a half-dozen letters. But there was still silence from behind the big mahogany door.

Snyder picked up another magazine and idly turned the pages, paying little attention to the words and pictures in front of him. Lieutenant Snyder was not happy.

He had brought the money with him—the usual twelve hundred dollars he had faithfully delivered every week for the past year and a half. But like so many other weeks, the past seven days had not been profitable for Snyder. His total collections had amounted to only thirteen hundred and eighty dollars. A skim of a hundred and eighty was damned thin for a bunco lieutenant. He'd made more than that when he was in uniform. And ten years ago, when he had been walking a beat, he had gotten almost twice that much in direct payments from Capone.

Twice during the past year Snyder had appealed to Christiansen for a reduction of his weekly quota. Christiansen had been sympathetic. The first time he suggested Snyder sweat it out a while and see if things picked up. The last time, three months ago, he'd listened again and said he'd talk to the boys upstairs. But nothing had happened.

The system was wrong, Snyder had decided. All the big operators in his precinct made their payments directly downtown—the bookies and policy-numbers spots, along with the high-priced whorehouses. The only things left for Snyder to hustle were the independents, the little fly-by-night operators. These were the free-lancers who took a bet now and then and generally didn't have any permanent location. Or the pimps who had a couple of girls working out of their own rooms. These types were hard to keep track of, and if he hustled them too much, they moved on to a new territory.

And then there were the pickpockets and grifters. They were even harder. Half of them were transients, and as quickly as he got a line on them, they would disappear and new ones would come in. It also involved a lot of streetwalking and night work, along with busting a few heads now and then. Snyder had no distaste for head busting, but it could be tiring.

The three thousand dollars he had collected from Johnny Hooker was a windfall that Snyder hoped would tide him over for a while. It was one of those little bonuses that came along now and then and made the whole thing worthwhile. He had expected to pick up another three thousand from Luther Coleman. But the nigger bastard had gotten himself pitched out of a third-story window before Snyder could get to him. And then Hooker's money turned out to be phony. Snyder had discovered it as quickly as he got home that night. The stuff looked like it had been made with a rubber stamp from a toy printing set.

After that Snyder had hoped to pick up a few hundred bucks by fingering Hooker to Lorrimer's people. But that hadn't worked out either. He had called Al Coombs at the cannery the next day and told him Hooker was the man they were looking for. "Yeah, we know that," Coombs had said, and asked where Hooker was. When Snyder couldn't tell him, Coombs called him a string of names and hung up on him. So he had gotten nothing for his troubles, not to mention the time he wasted when he could have been shaking somebody else down.

The fair way to solve his money problems, Snyder had decided, was for Christiansen to credit him with a part of the take from the big operators in his precinct. After all, Snyder did provide some protection for those people. The rougher he made it for the free-lance people the more business went to the organization people. So in a sense Snyder protected them from competition, and for this service he should receive some compensation. It was this logical analysis he intended to present to Captain Christiansen this morning. It was hard to imagine Christiansen refuting it, and Snyder had even considered the idea of asking for some sort of retroactive pay for his past services.

Whern the buzzer finally sounded on the secretary's desk, Snyder laid aside his magazine and looked up.

Christiansen's secretary was an attractive girl. A little thin for Snyder's tastes, but with good breasts and a pretty face. She listened on the phone and hung up. "You may go in now, Lieutenant." She smiled. Snyder went in.

"How's everything, Ray?"

"Pretty good, Chris." Snyder smiled and drew the packet of money from his coat as he crossed the room. He tossed it on the desk.

Christiansen was about ten years younger than Snyder—a tall, handsome, well-dressed man with blond hair and pale blue eyes. He had his feet on the desk, reading a newspaper. He glanced at the packet of money and set the newspaper aside. "Have a seat." He smiled.

For some reason Snyder always seemed to lose a little of his self-confidence when he entered this office. Christiansen was always friendly and sympathetic. But somehow the warm, paternal smile seemed to be hiding more than it revealed.

Christansen pulled open a lower drawer and dropped the money into a canvas bag. "Had a little trouble down your way last week, huh?" he said.

"Yeah." Snyder shrugged. "Nothing really that I can't handle." He had hoped this subject wouldn't come up. It made it awkward to shift the conversation to money. Snyder decided to wait a little.

"Yes," Christiansen said with a chuckle, "someone lifted eleven thousand dollars from one of Lorrimer's runners. I understand they threw one of them out a window."

"Yeah. An old colored guy."

"Yes, that's what I read in the paper." He chuckled again. "Lorrimer's people have the idea it was partly our fault. They figure we should have those street grifters under better control."

Christiansen was smiling at him as if he expected an answer. Snyder slid back in the chair. He shifted his weight to his elbows. "Yeah, well, they were just a couple of punks. These things happen, you know. I don't think they even knew the guy was a runner." He felt a trickle of cold perspiration drop from under his arm and slither down his ribs.

"I suppose not," Christiansen said.

Snyder shifted again. "The young guy—Hooker is his name—he dropped three thousand of the money on a roulette game over at Moffitt's." Why did he say that? It had no bearing on Lorrimer's complaint. The wrong thing always seemed to come out of his mouth when those pale blue eyes were fixed on him.

"That's what I heard," Christiansen said softly.

"I think I got a line on him, though," Snyder said.

"That's good." Christiansen nodded and looked around his desk. "There's something else I wanted to talk to you about," he said. "Starting next week, Ray, your quota is being raised to fifteen hundred."

For a split-second Snyder had thought he was going to say the quota had been lowered, that after all this time his protests had finally gotten some action. Instead it was as if the roof had suddenly collapsed on him. He was stunned. "What?" he managed to choke out.

Christiansen was nodding, anticipating the reaction. "I know it's tough, Ray, and I'm sorry. But this came right from the top. Everybody's being raised twenty-five percent." He smiled sadly. "It's election time, you know."

Snyder was at the edge of the chair again, his throat dry and his heart clamoring. "But, Jesus ... fifteen hundred!" He swallowed hard and shook his head. "My precinct just ain't got that kind of money, Chris. I mean, all the big money's going in direct. You know that. And there just ain't that much action on the streets. Hell, there's hardly no action at all. The system's all wrong. It isn't fair, Chris." His voice was cracking. What the hell was wrong with him, Snyder wondered. This wasn't the way he intended to present his case at all. He had worked it all out, and it was going to be a calm, reasonable discussion. "It's all wrong, Chris," he repeated.

Christiansen nodded again. He took a long, weary breath. "Ray," he said, "I'm going to give it to you straight. In the last two weeks, I've had three men in this office, sitting right where you are, all of them begging me for your territory. All young guys who want to move up. Maybe they don't realize the problems. Maybe they're just too ambitious. But the boys upstairs think maybe I oughta give one of them a chance. The pressure's really on, Ray. And frankly, after that unfortunate little incident with the runner last week, I don't know how long I can keep going to bat for you."

Snyder stared at him, feeling trapped, cheated, and betrayed all at once. After twenty-eight years he couldn't believe they would treat him like this. "That wasn't my fault, Chris," he said lamely. "You know that."

"It was your precinct."

"Yeah," Snyder said, "but fifteen hundred a week!"

Christiansen nodded grimly. He glanced at his watch and stood up. "Sorry, Ray," he said, "but you're just going to have to press a little harder."

Snyder looked up at him, at the expensive, neatly pressed suit, the silk shirt, and the manicured nails. He wondered how Christiansen had risen so fast in the department. "Yeah," he murmured vaguely. He rose and moved slowly toward the door, his mind reeling, his legs carrying him numbly forward.

"Nice to see you, Ray," Christiansen said behind him.

Snyder turned. The sympathetic smile was back on Christiansen's face. "Yeah," Snyder said, and tried to smile. "And thanks for goin' to bat for me."

"Sure."

Snyder trudged slowly out of the office and down the long hall, seeing nothing, lost in the gloom of his own hopelessness. His children were grown now. His boy had joined the army and was somewhere down in Texas. His daughter had gotten pregnant and married some kid up in Detroit. His wife. It had been ten years since Snyder and his wife had exchanged anything more than muttered grunts. And for twenty-eight years he had been working on the force, hoping he would get a break, that someday a little of the fat money would come his way. But it hadn't. And what little he had been able to scrape off the top disappeared as fast as he got it. What the hell was he going to do?

Snyder walked out on the street, and for five long minutes stood on the corner outside the police station. The wind snatched at his collar and hat brim, and he gazed absently at the mass of cars that stopped at the signal and then moved on. He saw truckdrivers and businessmen, black people and Italians, and housewives with cars full of kids. He paid no attention to any of them. And then he was looking at a young man in the back of a taxi. For almost half a minute his mind registered nothing. There was a gray suit and blue tie, a clean-cut, sandy-haired kid. Then, as if a hazy motion-picture film snapped suddenly into focus, Lieutenant Snyder was jolted abruptly to reality. He blinked at the figure in disbelief. The kid had a fresh haircut, and the clothes were new. But there was no question about it. It was Hooker.

For an instant Snyder was immobilized with indecision. People were jostling past him on the sidewalk. In the street the signal had changed, and the cars were pulling away. The taxi was already roaring through the intersection. Snyder stared hopelessly at it for a second and then looked back toward the police building. A squad car was at the curb, a cop reading a newspaper behind the wheel. Snyder bolted for it, his coattails flying behind him.

From the hotel, Hooker walked a block west to Wabash, and then two blocks south before he stepped into a phone booth.

Twist answered on the third ring.

"Twist? This is Hooker. I told Lorrimer the tale. He wants to see you."

"All right. What time?"

"We'll be by a little after four. Stay inside. I'll come in and get you. And you can be a little hard on him. He's talking money."

"Big money?"

"I think so."

"Okay, tootsie," Twist said, and the phone clicked off.

That was that, Hooker thought. He replaced the receiver on the hook and turned to open the door. Then he froze, his heart leaping violently in his chest.

Pressed that close to the glass, any face would have startled Hooker. But Lieutenant Snyder's pockmarked smirk paralyzed him. He was trapped, and Snyder knew it. The grin grew broader and the eyes narrower as the cop slowly drew out his gun.

Hooker flattened against the wall behind him as the pistol came up and leveled itself directly at his face. Jesus, was he going to kill him right here in broad daylight?

Hooker winced as the first crash came. But Snyder had not fired. He was lifting the pistol again and again, pounding it against the window, shattering the glass into deadly splinters.

Hooker felt the sting of glass slivers in his cheek. He lifted his hand to protect himself, and then dropped to the floor of the booth as the pounding continued. "You little bastard!" Snyder was yelling. "I'm gonna cut off your balls and stuff 'em up . . ."

The words ended with a crash. His back braced against the rear of the booth, Hooker thrust his legs forward with all his strength. He felt the door crack heavily against Snyder, and he heard the startled grunt as the lieutenant hit the ground. Then Hooker was running.

In one movement he rolled forward out of the booth and came to his feet. Without looking back, he took off, his legs flying beneath him, the accumulation of adrenalin seeming to propel him effortlessly across the street, around the corner, and then down the next block. Without waiting for a break in traffic, he veered off across the next street and darted into a half-demolished building.

At the top of the third flight of stairs he finally stopped. Gasping for breath, he held the banister and peered down the stairwell, wondering for a moment if Snyder had even bothered to chase him. But Snyder quickly came into the building and stopped just inside the door, the gun still in his hand.

There was an open door behind Hooker. Beyond it the wall had been torn down, and Hooker could see daylight. He moved through the door, locked it behind him, and then paused, peering down at the alley below. It was a thirty-foot drop. He looked at the fire escape on the building across from him. There was about a ten-foot gap. He moved out to the farthest edge of solid flooring. He hesitated a second and jumped.

He caught the iron railing, dangling in midair for a moment. Then he got a firm grip with both hands and pulled himself up and over. If Snyder had made it to the third floor, he still hadn't gotten the door open. Hooker stepped back. He lifted his foot and jammed it into the window, sending glass clattering to the floor inside. He undid the latch, and went in.

Coming out of the front door of the building, Hooker smiled and walked briskly eastward, touching his cheek for the first time. There was dried blood all the way down his chin and neck. The half-inch splinter of glass was still embedded in his cheek. Hooker stopped walking. He carefully grasped the splinter and pulled it out. He tossed it aside and moved on again, dabbing his face with a handkerchief.

"Why didn't you tell me about Snyder before?" Gondorff asked as Billie washed the wound with a piece of gauze.

Hooker shrugged. "I thought I'd lost him."

"Well, you found him again," Gondorff said irritably, "and sooner or later, we're gonna have to do something about it."

"Aw, he's just a cheap shakedown artist. He's been chasin' me for years."

"How much does he want?"

"Three grand."

Gondorff grunted. "You call that cheap, huh?"

"Don't worry about it." Hooker smiled. "I'll stay clear. I got his number now."

Gondorff nodded. "Yeah."

Kid Twist and J. J. Singleton pulled up in front of the telegraph office at twenty minutes to four. Twist was driving. He wore a pair of paint-stained coveralls, completely obscuring the brown business suit he wore underneath. A house painter's cap was pushed to the back of his head. Singleton wore a similar outfit, and on the side of the panel truck was the lettering: "CLAYTON BROS., CUSTOM PAINTING AND DECORATING."

Business was slow for the Clayton brothers. They had been delighted to earn thirty dollars by renting out the coveralls, truck, and painting equipment for three hours.

From the back of the truck Twist and Singleton gathered armloads of brushes, paint tarpaulins, and a stepladder. Loading themselves up, they marched into the reception room of the telegraph office. The receptionist was more than surprised to see them.

"Excuse me," Twist said, "we're here to paint Mr. Harmon's office." He handed the girl a paper authorizing the job.

"Mr. Harmon's office?" the girl said hesitantly. "Can you hold on for just a second?"

Twist smiled, and the girl disappeared through a door.

Singleton had gotten the authorization form from the painters who had last redecorated the telegraph office in Evanston. He told them he was from New York, investigating procurement precedures of the company, and if they didn't mind, he would like to look over the purchase order for the job. They didn't mind. When they brought out the form, he frowned suspiciously at it and asked if he could take it along with him. They insisted they had been involved in no hanky-panky, that the job had been done at a fair price with no kickbacks or collusion. Singleton assured them he had no doubts about their honesty or the quality of their work. He was interested only in the technical aspects of internal procedures. When he returned to Chicago, it was a simple matter to have a printer copy the form, and for Twist to forge the proper signature.

Mr. Harmon came out of the office with the paper in his hand, as bewildered as the girl had been. He was a slender man with rimless glasses, and a miniature telegraph key on his tie clip. "Brigham signed it, all right," he said. "I can't understand why he didn't tell me about it."

"Aw, he's like all them supervisors," Twist said. "They think they're too good for regular people. He says he was in here a while ago and the place was a mess."

"Oh?" Harmon said. He glanced around, a little alarmed.

Twist and Singleton picked up their equipment and moved toward the office. "We'll try to hurry so we don't keep you out of your office too long." Twist smiled.

"In my office? Can't I work in there while you're painting?"

Singleton shook his head. "Look, pal, we gotta cover the floor, the furniture, everything, so we don't spill on nothin'. Now, if you wanta sit in there with a tarp over your head, you're welcome to it."

Harmon started to open his mouth, then thought better of it. "All right. How long will you be?"

"An hour or two at the most." Twist shrugged. "We do good work. Anything you want to get out of there before we start?"

"No," Harmon said, "I guess not."

As quickly as they had closed the door, Twist pulled off his coveralls. While Singleton spread traps around, he placed a framed picture on the desk—a photograph showing himself, a woman, and three small children. Singleton dipped his brush in a bucket and started sloshing paint on one of the walls, as Twist checked the back door. It opened into a narrow alley, about a hundred feet back from the street. He was pleased. He closed the door and sat down with his feet on Harmon's desk. "That's beautiful work, J. J." he said.

"You done?" the girl at Angie's Diner asked Hooker.

Hooker had eaten the gristly ham, but he had taken only two bites out of the eggs and then pushed the plate aside. He had come to the diner early, at twenty to four, and watched the street outside for Lorrimer's arrival while he ate.

"Yeah," Hooker said. "I guess I shoulda had the meatloaf."

The girl shrugged and picked up the plate. "It isn't any better." She dropped the mess clattering into a bin that was already full. She was a new girl, a slim, tough-looking cookie with her black hair pulled back into a bun. The small scar under her left eye was interesting. Hooker wondered who had given it to her and why.

"Where's June today?" he asked.

The girl didn't seem much interested in June, or anything else, for that matter. She leaned over the counter, figuring Hooker's bill; indifferent to the exposure of her loosely brassiered breasts. For such a slim girl they were good-sized.

"She don't work here no more," she said. "I'm fillin' in for a couple of days." She straightened and tossed the slip in front of Hooker. "Till I can get a train outa here."

"What's your name?"

"Loretta," she said, as if she didn't care much about that either. She banged some more plates into the bin.

"Where ya goin'?"

"I don't know," she said, and headed for the kitchen. "Depends on what train I get on."

Hooker watched her disappear into the back. He tossed a dollar on the counter, finished his coffee, and picked up a couple of toothpicks as he went out the door.

Lorrimer's big black Packard rolled up to the curb two minutes later. Hooker flicked away his toothpick and hopped into the back seat.

Lorrimer was in a dark business suit, a big diamond sparkling on his pinkie. "What happened to your face?" he muttered.

Hooker smiled. "Aw, I had a little fight with a raggle down on Thirteenth. She got me with her ring."

Lorrimer shook his head and laughed.

At the telegraph office Hooker told the driver to park around the corner. "We'd better go to the back door," he said as they got out. Lorrimer followed him, glancing suspiciously around as they moved down the alley.

Hooker knocked softly. A chair squeaked inside. There were footsteps, and Twist opened the door.

"Les," Hooker said, "I got Mr. Lorrimer here with me. He wants to see you a second."

A sudden flash of anger crossed Twist's face. "What the hell's the matter with you?" he said, glancing over his shoulder. "We coulda met at a club or something."

Lorrimer eyes were searching the office.

"I thought it would be good for him to see the setup," Hooker said.

"Yeah," Twist shot back in a hushed voice, "and great for everybody to see you around here." He sighed. "Well, we can't talk here. They're having the place painted. Just a second."

Twist left the door open and went to the desk, flipping a key on the intercom. The framed picture was clearly visible on the desk, and Hooker saw Lorrimer taking it all in.

"Miss Barnes," Twist said, "I'm going home a little

early today. Tell anyone who calls that they can reach me in the morning. Thank you."

Twist glanced irritably at his watch as he moved quickly to the door. "Okay," he said, "Let's get out of here."

As quickly as the door closed, Singleton tossed his brush in the paint bucket and moved across to the back of the office. He opened the door a crack. Behind him the other doorknob rattled. There was a firm knock, and Mr. Harmon's muffled voice came through. "Sir? Hello? Would you kindly open this door, please?"

Singleton watched until the Packard pulled away and disappeared. Then he grabbed the portrait from the desk and hurried out the back door and around to the truck.

Twist insisted they drive at least a mile away from the telegraph office before they talked. "It was a dumb thing to do, Carver," he said.

"Yeah," Hooker said. "I guess I shoulda called you first."

Lorrimer sat in silence, his eyes half-closed, as if mulling over his impressions of the telegraph office and the man sitting next to him. "That place okay?" he finally said.

A rundown Chinese restaurant with a gilt dragon in front was coming up half a block ahead of them.

"Yeah," Twist said.

The driver pulled over. When they were inside, he stationed himself just inside the door, and the others slid into a dark booth at the side.

Twist listened and then empathically shook his head when Hooker explained that Lorrimer wanted to make another test bet.

"Can't do it," he said flatly. "There's telegraph inspectors all over the place, and I got seven hundred and fifty grand coming in from the coast. I'm not gonna blow the whole setup for a lousy test." He gave

Hooker a look of disgust. "We'll get somebody else to do our betting."

Hooker looked at Lorrimer. He was pushing a salt shaker from one hand to the other. "I could come up with the seven hundred and fifty grand," he said quietly, "if I had a reason to."

Twist snorted. "But who says you will? I got a guy I can depend on. He's liquidating everything he has for this. Hell, you wouldn't even give Carver his money back."

Lorrimer smiled faintly and shrugged. "I need more proof, that's all. Anybody can get lucky once."

"On an eight-to-one shot?" Twist said. "To hell with you, pal. We'll keep the deal we got."

Lorrimer considered this, the eyes half-closing again, the poker player weighing the strength of his hand. His decision came quickly, the voice suddenly hard, ready to deal.

"If it works again tomorrow," he said, "I'll have a million cash here by noon the next day. I get sixty, you two get forty."

Twist appeared startled by Lorrimer's decisiveness. He squirmed a little, his voice weakening. "We were getting fifty from our guy," he said.

"A week's a long time, friend," Lorrimer said. "Anything can happen." He smiled. "All of it bad."

"He's right, Les," Hooker said.

Twist chewed the inside of his lip and looked at Hooker. "Yeah," he said glumly, "and what if we make the test play tomorrow and then he doesn't come up with the million? We risk our whole operation for nothing."

"So what do we know about our guy?" Hooker protested. "He says a week, but who knows if it's a month? Lorrimer here's a banker. He can get the dough with no questions asked."

Twist took a deep breath and let it out slowly.

"Your friend's right, you know," Lorrimer said quietly.

Twist was unable to deny the arguments. And they were both against him. "All right," he finally said. "Be at the drugstore at one o'clock." "I'll give you all three places this time—win, place and show. That should be proof enough for you."

Lorrimer nodded. He smiled over at Hooker as if congratulating him on his part in the victory. Hooker returned the smile.

Hooker was the last to slide out of the booth. They were halfway back to the telegraph office before it finally came to him.

There was something strange in that Chinese restaurant, something that had scratched faintly at his memory, partially distracting him all through the conversation. But he had ignored it at the time, concentrating on the role he was playing.

Aside from the kids in leather jackets who were playing the pinball machines in the back, there had been only two or three customers in the place. And then a dark man with a newspaper had come in and sat down in a booth across from them. They had all glanced at him and continued talking. It was not until a couple of minutes later, when the man was served coffee and lifted the cup, that the uneasy question arose in Hooker's mind. The man wore a black glove, and his middle finger was missing. There was nothing startling about that, except that somewhere in the past day or so Hooker had glimpsed that same hand. And it was not until he was back in the car, sitting silently between Lorrimer and Twist, that it came to him.

It was when he had called Twist earlier in the day, just before Snyder had trapped him in the phone booth. While he was dialing he had noticed a car pull to the curb across the street. The driver had not gotten out. But after Hooker bashed Snyder and barreled out of the phone booth, the man *was* out of the car. Hooker paid no attention as he roared past him. But for some reason the fleeting glimpse of that gloved hand resting on the car door had stayed with him. At the time he had other things on his mind.

But now, as he put the two incidents together, Hooker wondered. Was it strictly chance that the same man had twice been in the same place as he? Or that two different men had the same finger missing, and wore black gloves, and he'd seen them both on the same day?

Hooker knew he was a lousy gambler. But he didn't believe much in million-to-one shots. Jesus, he thought, just give him two more days.

V. The Shutout

The coffee and doughnuts turned sour as quickly as they slid into Snyder's stomach. He felt the burning sensation and the faint pressure of gas building up. But he continued chewing, stuffing the last of the sugary dough into his mouth, and washing it down with the hot, liquid.

He knew he would get Hooker. Sooner or later he would run into him again. And next time, he wouldn't fool around. If necessary, he would shoot the bastard before he let him get away.

What galled Snyder was seeing Hooker wearing a new suit, riding in a taxi, and going into the Sherman Hotel. Where had he gotten the money, and what the hell was he up to? Snyder knew Hooker had dropped four thousand at the roulette table in Moffitt's. Had he kept the whole eleven thousand he and Coleman lifted from Lorrimer's runner? Maybe they hadn't divided it before Coleman was killed. Thinking about it sent another spurt of burning acid into Snyder's stomach. He tossed a dime on the counter, finished his coffee and headed for the door.

In the meantime, he reflected bitterly, he had to squeeze another three hundred bucks out of the crud that worked the streets of his precinct. Either that or ... He didn't want to think about what would happen if he didn't come up with the money. Would he be back in uniform, or would they just freeze him out completely? No, he knew too much for them to just drop him. They wouldn't dare do that. They wouldn't risk his going to the newspapers or the feds and spilling his guts. The thought comforted him a little.

Jesus, Snyder thought, he would drive himself crazy thinking about things like this. He had to stop. To hell with it, he would get the money.

He was standing in front of a newsstand now. People were hurrying past him, grabbing newspapers on their way to work, their collars turned up against the gusty wind.

Snyder looked over the headlines. "FDR PROMISES PROSPERITY." Shit, Snyder thought. His gaze shifted to Pinky, who was handing out papers, hurriedly making change out of a cigar box. When things weren't so rushed, Pinky took horse bets for a bookie over on Forty-fifth Street. The bookie was a big operator and sent his juice money directly to City Hall. Snyder wondered if maybe Pinky held a few of the bets himself, didn't pass them along. Maybe Pinky had a few sidelines. Like pimping, or selling policy numbers. Snyder smiled. Or better yet, maybe Pinky *didn't* have any sidelines. Maybe Pinky might be interested in some kind of partnership to develop a few.

"Snyder?"

The hard voice coming from behind him startled Snyder, as if someone were listening in on his private thoughts. He turned sharply, catching his breath.

The two men were huge, towering half a foot above him. They were both wearing white skimmers and tan trench coats. One of them had a wallet in his hand. He flipped it open, revealing a badge and an identification card.

"FBI," he said coldly, "We'd like a few words with you."

Snyder was speechless, his heart suddenly hammering frantically in his chest. The man's wallet disappeared, and both of them stepped back, gesturing him toward the open door of a car next to the curb. Snyder moved hesitantly. He licked his lips. "Listen, I got work to do. I can't . . ."

The man moved him along, guiding him gently by the elbow toward the back seat. "It won't take long," he said.

They drove in silence, the two FBI men seated in front, gazing impassively forward. In the back, Snyder racked his brain trying to remember anything he had done that might have violated federal laws. There was nothing, except maybe back in prohibition days. And the statute of limitations would protect him there. Income tax? No, it couldn't be income tax. He hadn't made enough money. Not unless they counted all the collections he made and passed on. But they couldn't get him for that. Could they? Jesus, Snyder thought.

They had driven west toward Cicero and then headed south. They were slowing now, turning into the loading ramp of an abandoned warehouse.

The driver opened Snyder's door and nodded toward the steps leading into the building. "In there."

The man led him through a shipping office and into a corner of the warehouse cluttered by empty crates. Two more men wearing white skimmers and trench coats were seated on boxes. A third in shirtsleeves stood with his hands on his hips, gazing contemptuously at him.

"Have a seat, Snyder," he said. "I'm special agent Polk. These are agents Broyles and McCormick."

Snyder glanced around at the stony-faced group.

"Hey, what is this? I got a beat to run. You guys ain't got no jurisdic—"

The guy named Polk waved him into silence. "Sit down and shut up, will ya, Snyder? Try not to live up to all my expectations."

Snyder sat down. Polk lit a cigarette, took a deep drag, and started pacing. "We were told you know a guy named Hooker."

Snyder glanced around at the others. They were all looking at him, like he was some kind of worm.

"Well," Polk demanded, "do you know him, or don't ya?"

"Yeah." Snyder nodded. "I know him. But I don't know where he is."

"Well, we do," Polk said. "He's workin' for a guy named Henry Gondorff. Ring any bells?"

Snyder relaxed a little. Apparently they had nothing on him. Something bigger was in the works. "Of course," he said a little cockily. "Every bunco man in the country knows Gondorff."

Polk paced some more. He took another pull on the cigarette. "We got word he's runnin' a con on the North Side here. We been trying to nail him for a year now. But nothin's gonna stick in court unless we catch him cold. What we want you to do is pick up Hooker for us."

That was funny, Snyder thought. The great FBI wanted him to do their work for them. "Why don't ya pick him up yourself?"

Polk ignored the insolent tone. "Because," he said, "the stoolies are used to you bothering him. If word gets around that feds are involved too, Gondorff'll fold up the whole thing. We're not even letting the police in on this. And if you keep your mouth shut and do a job for us, there'll be some bucks in it for ya."

Snyder smiled to himself. This was getting more interesting. "And there might be a few bucks for me if I *didn't* keep my mouth shut, too."

Polk stopped pacing and stared at him. Then he smiled and slowly nodded. "You really know all the angles, don't ya, Snyder?"

Snyder shrugged. "A man has to make a living."

"Okay." Polk nodded, and paced again. "I understand this Hooker kid owes you some money. How much?"

"Six grand," Snyder said without hesitation.

Polk threw him a sharp glance. "C'mon, Snyder, we can't throw around that kind of money. And your chances of getting it from Hooker are zero. How much?"

Snyder took a deep breath, quickly weighing the situation. If he dropped too low, they would figure him for a small-time operator, maybe worth nothing to them. And Gondorff was a big man. Snyder had vague recollections of Gondorff having bitten a senator somewhere down south. And the senator had been putting heat on the FBI ever since. Yeah, he thought, they'd pay.

"Four thousand," he said. "That's bottom."

Polk threw away his cigarette. "You're a fucking thief, Snyder. We oughta just lock you up."

"Sure. And then you can go out and pick up Hooker yourself."

Snyder saw the jaw clamp tight. He had them.

"Okay," Polk finally said. "We'll fix it somehow. McCormick, make a note of that. Four grand for Lieutenant Snyder."

Snyder watched the agent fish out a small pad and make notations. He smiled to himself. They were really desperate. The old senator must have lit a big fire under J. Edgar Hoover's ass.

"That's all I gotta do?" Snyder asked. "Pick up Hooker for ya?"

"That's all. And maybe give us a little help when we make the arrest."

That was all right, too. Snyder thought. A front-page picture of him and a couple of FBI men throwing handcuffs on a big-time con man like Gondorff would make them sit up and take notice at City Hall. Even *those* bastards didn't want to screw around with the feds. He looked over at Polk.

"What the hell good is Hooker to ya?"

"He's gonna set up Gondorff for us."

Snyder shook his head. "I know that kid. He'll never do it."

Polk looked at him and smiled. "I think he will."

"You understand what we're gonna do?" Gondorff asked.

"Yeah," Hooker said. "J. J. told me you're gonna shut him out."

Gondorff nodded. "He's betting fourteen thousand. We haven't got enough to cover it. He's gonna be hot about it," Gondorff said. "But it oughta give him a bigger appetite for tomorrow." He gave Hooker a pat on the back and moved away from the bar, glancing around at the crowd.

It was a quarter to one, and they were setting up again, spreading racing forms and drinks and ashtrays around while Eddie Niles handed out phony money to the bettors. The Englishman was gone. Curly Jackson had shed the Van Dyke and monocle and was now the aging sport, fresh off his polo pony and wearing white pants and a dashing blue blazer.

Hooker turned back to his coffee. He was tired. Thinking about the four-fingered man with the black glove had gotten to him last night. Every creak of the wind had brought him bolt upright in his bed. There was something about that man—a cool efficiency he had never feared from Riley and Cole. Even in their pictures they had the dumb look of gorillas—too dumb to catch him if he was careful. But the four-fingered man seemed to have no trouble finding him.

"Ten minutes," Gondorff shouted. "Billie, you'd better get some fresh drinks on those tables."

Hooker finished his coffee and put the empty cup under the bar.

Amon Lorrimer looked at the big clock over the soda fountain and checked it with his own watch. Both said ten minutes to one. He took another sip of the coffee in front of him. It was terrible. He pushed the cup away and picked up a knife, pinging it absently against a salt shaker.

Even if the horses came in one-two-three today, he was still undecided about making a million-dollar bet. He had called Joe Leonard in New York this morning and told him to get the money ready just in case. But it was going to be tricky. Leonard would have to gather all the cash they had in all the banks, and then juggle a few checks with other banks to make up the balance. If Lorrimer gave him the word, a messenger would bring the money by plane first thing in the morning. Then, after he collected on the bet, Lorrimer would have to hustle the million back to New York by the time the banks opened the next morning. Even at that, they were risking the unexpected arrival of a bank examiner, or the possibility of one of the other banks making a quick demand on a check. But they could probably stall them for the necessary twenty-four hours. It wouldn't be the first time Lorrimer had floated paper for a day or two.

Also, Leonard told him, Moran was getting impatient. Nitti was getting hit so hard, it looked like he might make a deal with the North Side. And if Lorrimer didn't come up with the money quick, Moran was going to throw in with them too. That would leave Lorrimer by himself, a fat pig ready for slaughter.

"Tell him he's got a deal, and we'll have the dough there day after tomorrow," Lorrimer said.

"You really gonna go for it?"

"Maybe."

"Should I send over some beef to help out Nitti?"

"Naw, let him sweat a little. Tell him we're bringing in some troops from Chicago and the coast and they'll be there in a couple of days. I want him on his knees when we're ready to move. And another thing," Lorrimer said as an afterthought, "have the boys make a couple of hits on Moran's spots. Make it look like North Side action. Understand? If Moran gets nervous, maybe his price will drop a little."

Leonard had understood.

It looked like there wasn't much choice for Lorrimer now. He either made the move and wrapped up New York, or they squeezed him out. And if he made the move, it would have to be decisive. He would need more men, and more money than the half-million Moran wanted. The money could come from Shaw's bookie joint. He wondered how much cash Shaw really had. From the action around the place, had to have three or four million available.

Lorrimer tapped the salt shaker some more, and then looked up quickly as the phone jangled above him. He reached up for the receiver and put it to his ear.

"Feature race. Saratoga." the voice said. "Wrecking Crew at four to one, Grand Theft place, and Made to Order show." The phone clicked and buzzed.

One of his bodyguards waited outside, and the other two fanned out in the crowd after Hooker opened the door. There were four men already standing in line at the betting window. Lorrimer recognized a few faces from his previous visit, but there were a lot of new ones. He didn't see Gondorff anywhere. Lorrimer looked up front, where Niles was slowly counting out a stack of bills. "C'mon," he said, "let's hurry it up there."

The speaker above his head crackled. "One minute till post time at Saratoga."

There were two men in front of him now. The man at the window was betting twenty-five thousand on Grand Theft. Lorrimer pulled out his fourteen thousand dollars and got it ready. The man immediately in front of him stepped forward. He was a seedy-looking character with no tie and a day's growth of stubble on his face.

"Thirty thousand on Wrecking Crew," he said, and began counting out bills. His hands were trembling.

"C'mon, for Christ's sake," Lorrimer said.

The man turned and looked at him. He frowned and began counting all over again.

"Good afternoon, ladies and gentlemen," the speaker suddenly rasped. "This is Arnold Rowe, your track announcer for the hundred-thousand-dollar Fairfield Stakes at Saratoga. A mile and three-eighths for three-year-olds and up. The horses are in the gate."

The man finally turned away. Lorrimer stepped quickly forward and tossed down the money. "Fourteen thousand on Wrecking Crew."

Niles was snapping a rubber band around the money from the previous bettor. He looked up just as the announcer said, "They're off and running!"

Niles shook his head. "I'm sorry, sir. We can't take bets after the race is started." He pointed to a sign above the cage.

Lorrimer didn't look at the sign. He glared angrily at Niles, and then over at Gondorff, who had strolled up to the counter.

"Don't take it so hard, pal," Gondorff said. "You probably woulda lost it anyway."

Grabbing his money, Lorrimer turned and pushed roughly past two customers toward the bar. The stupid bastard, he thought. If Gondorff had any brains, he'd spend ten bucks for another betting clerk.

"And they're going around the first turn," the announcer said. "Wrecking Crew is in the lead by half a length, Grand Theft is second by one, His Dandy by a half, followed by Change of Heart, Back Flip, Made to Order, and High Ground is trailing."

"What would you like, sir?" a voice said.

Lorrimer looked across the bar. The bartender was leaning toward him with a questioning smile.

"Nothing," Lorrimer muttered.

The seedy-looking man with no tie was seated next to him. "Who you got?" he asked.

Lorrimer looked at him and turned away. "Wrecking Crew."

"Me too. I hope he can hold on. Maybe it's our day."

Lorrimer nodded feebly. The horses were going down the backstretch. Wrecking Crew was in front by four lengths now. Hooker moved toward Lorrimer through the crowd, bringing empty glasses to the bar again.

"What happened?" he murmured as he reached the glasses across.

"I didn't get the bet down."

Hooker looked up sharply. "Oh, Jesus!" he said, and glanced off toward the betting window. When he turned back, he shrugged and forced a smile. "Well, at least you can see if we called it right."

Lorrimer just grunted and looked off at the crowd. The horses were coming down the stretch, Wrecking Crew five lengths ahead now. The screaming began. Most of the bettors seemed to be for Grand Theft, who was moving up a little. He didn't have much chance of making it. The man next to Lorrimer had his eyes closed, pleading in quiet desperation for Wrecking Crew to hang in there.

"It's Wrecking Crew, Grand Theft, and Made to Order." Singleton was saying. "They're coming down to the wire, and it's Wrecking Crew an easy winner by five lengths, Grand Theft is second by a nose, and Made to Order."

Lorrimer suddenly felt himself jolted. There was a hand on each of his shoulders, shaking him violently. "We won! We won!" the seedy-looking guy was screaming. "I won a hundred and twenty thousand bucks! You hear that?"

Lorrimer pushed the hands roughly away and headed for the door.

"Time for the mile and three-eighths," the speaker droned, "was two-thirteen and four-fifths."

His bodyguard had the door open, and Lorrimer strode through. Hooker was waiting in the alley.

"You tell your friend," Lorrimer said, "that I'll have the money here by post time tomorrow. We'll take the first race where the odds are five to one or better. And you make sure I get to the window this time."

Hooker gaped at him. "How'm I gonna do that?"

"I don't know," Lorrimer growled. "Figure something out." He stormed off toward the Packard, the two bodyguards scurrying after him. Hooker smiled and went back into the store.

They were all waiting in silence. Then Twist's buzzer sounded, and everybody relaxed.

"How's it look?" Gondorff asked.

Hooker smiled. "He says he'll have the million tomorrow."

Gondorff nodded, satisfied. He poured himself a drink at the bar and downed it quickly.

"Henry," Hooker asked, "how you gonna work it?"

Gondorff took a long breath and rubbed his chin, considering the question. "I don't know yet. If he was an ordinary rube playin' for a couple of grand, we'd just give him the wrong horse. Or maybe pay him off with phony money. But Lorrimer's got too much muscle for that kind of stunt. No, we gotta make it stick with him." He looked up and smiled. "Don't worry about it, kid. I'll think of something."

After they cleaned up, Hooker changed his clothes and left. He walked down Loomis Street for a while and turned east on Roosevelt. There was nothing left to do now. At this time tomorrow it would be all over. They would have Lorrimer's money. Gondorff, Twist, Singleton and Eddie Niles would head directly for the train station and scatter all over the country. He should probably do the same thing. But he had no idea where he could go. The farthest he had ever been in his life was the trip to Pittsburgh. And then the only thing he'd seen was the inside of the terminal before they boarded the train back to Chicago.

He wondered what Eirie had been up to lately, and if he had been fingered too. But it would be too risky to go back to the old neighborhood and start asking questions.

He stopped in front of a movie theater and stared vaguely at the posters for a while. It was a double feature—*Make Way for a Lady*, with Herbert Marshall, and *Reckless*, starring Jean Harlow and William Powell. He bought a ticket and found his way down to the front row.

Herbert Marshall was a widower, and his daughter was trying to find a new wife for him. Hooker gazed up at the grainy figures for ten minutes and fell asleep.

It was almost dark when he came out. He headed east again, until he reached the lakefront, and then went to Angie's Diner. He had meatloaf, and as Loretta had told him, it was no better than the ham and eggs.

"Haven't found a train leaving town yet, huh?" Hooker said when she refilled his coffeecup.

"Not yet."

"Maybe you oughta try a bus."

She walked away, filling cups at the other end of the counter.

Hooker waited until she was at the cash register and went up to pay his tab. "What time you get off work?"

"Two A.M."

"You doin' anything tonight?"

"Yeah. Sleepin'."

"Where you live?"

For a half-second she looked at him as if considering the proposal. Then she smiled wearily and headed back along the counter. "Forget it," she said.

Hooker walked aimlessly for another half-hour and then headed for home.

The landlady was standing in the little vestibule with a mop and a bucket. Apparently a bum had puked in the doorway, and she was giving the whole place a Clorox bath. She gave a Hooker a tight-lipped glance as if he was one of the vast army of people put on this earth to aggravate her.

"Any messages?" Hooker asked.

"Nope. No calls, no messages."

Hooker watched her slosh the mop around, and then headed for the elevator.

"Don't you make no noise when you go up there, now," she called after him. "I rented that room next to yours today. To a real gentleman."

Hooker paused and then continued to the elevator.

"Paid a whole month in advance, he did."

Hooker smiled. He had paid for only a week. The elevator was in use somewhere above. Hooker pressed the button and looked curiously back at the landlady. He moved back toward the vestibule. "Mrs. Bascombe, did this man by any chance ask for that specific room?"

"I don't see what business it is of yours. He asked for a room on the third floor at the front. I showed him the two rooms I had vacant and he took that one."

"What's his name?"

She stopped swinging the mop and squinted suspiciously at him. "Brown," she said, "Mr. C. G. Brown."

It might be nothing. Thousands of people rented rooms every day in Chicago. And if it were Riley or Cole, why would they bother getting a room next to his? If they knew where he lived, they could easily lay for him outside. Then another thought crossed his mind. "Mrs. Bascombe, does this man happen to have a finger missing on his right hand?"

Her mouth tightened, as if Hooker had beat her at some game they were playing. "Well," she said huffily, "I don't know that it's his *right* hand. All I know is that Mr. Brown is a perfect gentleman, and—"

"Mrs. Bascombe," Hooker interrupted, his heart suddenly accelerating, "is he up there now?"

"How should *I* know? I don't run no hotel here, where people check in and out every minute with ..."

Hooker was already past the elevator, heading for the back. He bounded quickly down the three steps, pushed open the door, and was in the alley. He glanced to his right, and then, turning toward the street, stopped abruptly.

"Not a muscle," Lieutenant Snyder said viciously, "or you're going to be splattered all over this alley."

Snyder was playing no games this time. The pistol was held high, leveled directly at Hooker's nose. "Turn around," he said, "and put your hands behind your back."

Hooker did as he was told. He heard the clinking of handcuffs. Then they were on his wrists. He winced as Snyder squeezed them down to their tightest notch. Snyder snatched his wallet from his pocket, pulled out the money and quickly searched for secret compartments. There weren't any.

"Eighty-five bucks, huh?" Snyder said. He put the money in his own pocket and shoved the wallet back into Hooker's. "For a big-time con man, that's not much, Hooker."

"It's enough for a third-rate cop."

Snyder's fist caught him on the ear, and Hooker sprawled face-forward onto the pavement.

"Now, get your ass over in that car."

Hooker maneuvered his legs under him. He got to his feet, shook his head in an effort to stop the ringing, and walked to the car. Snyder opened the door shoved him into the back seat. Then he opened another pair of handcuffs, pulled Hooker's hands down to the floor, and locked him to the springs under the front seat. He slammed the door, and drove off.

Hooker shifted, getting himself as comfortable as possible, wondering what the hell Snyder was up to. He certainly wouldn't be taking him to the station to book him. There wasn't any money in that. To Lorrimer, maybe?

The car swerved. Hooker pulled as hard as he could in an effort to break the cuffs loose from under the seat but they were solidly anchored. He lay back and closed his eyes, hoping the next face he saw wouldn't be Lorrimer's.

The car finally stopped at the old warehouse where Snyder had been taken earlier in the day. With Snyder prodding him, Hooker stumbled forward through the darkness and into a dimly-lit crate room where Polk and three of his men were waiting.

Polk was in his shirtsleeves, a pistol holstered under his arm.

"Hello, Mr. Hooker," he said. "I'm special agent Polk, FBI. Take the cuffs off him, Snyder."

Snyder unlocked the cuffs, and Hooker rubbed his wrists. The FBI. What the hell would the FBI want with him? And why were they working with a sleazy bastard like Snyder?

"Have a seat, Hooker," Polk said. "You want a drink or something?"

Hooker glanced down at a crate next to him. He remained standing. "No."

Polk lit another cigarette. It was his style. He leaned an arm casually on a stack of crates. "We want to talk to you about Henry Gondorff."

Hooker's heart jumped. He'd forgotten about Gondorff's trouble with the feds. "Don't know him."

Polk smiled and looked thoughtfully at his cigarette. "You know, that's a bad lie for a man who's due to take a fall. Lieutenant Snyder here says you done a lotta griftin' in this town."

"Lieutenant Snyder doesn't know shit."

For a second Polk looked like he was going to laugh. Instead he rubbed his nose a couple of times, until he was under control again.

"You got nothin' on me," Hooker said.

"We'll get it. And if we can't, we'll just make it up. Grand larceny, extortion..." He paused for emphasis. "Counterfeiting. Anything you want."

Hooker knew Polk could do what he said. If they really wanted to, they could put him away for life.

"All you gotta do," Polk said casually, "is tell us when Gondorff's gonna play his chump.

"We come in at the sting, make the pinch, and you walk out free as a bird. No questions, no court appearance, nothing. May even square things for you with Snyder here."

"No," Hooker said flatly.

"You wanna sit in the can for twenty years? No parole? We might even arrange an ill-considered escape for you. You know where that leaves you, don't you, Hooker?"

Shit, Hooker thought. It was easy for them. Too easy. He looked sharply at the man. "You make me puke, Polk."

Polk smiled. "Then we got a deal, huh?" He gazed at Hooker through a full minute of silence, waiting. "Whatd'ya say, kid?"

Hooker took a deep breath. He eased down on the crate next to him rubbing his wrists again, his eyes on the floor. "Will you wait until the chump is played?"

"Hell, yes," Polk said. "We don't care about the mark. He deserves what he gets."

Hooker looked up. "I mean completely played. Until he's beat, and the score is taken. You come in before we beat him, and I'll kill him. You'll have a tough time explaining that, won't ya?"

"All right, Hooker," Polk said, "but we're gonna keep you under twenty-four-hour surveillance. You try to take it on the lam, and we'll shoot you down on sight."

Hooker nodded. "Just so long as I get to finish the play."

"Okay. When does it happen?"

"I don't know yet," Hooker said. "It hasn't been decided."

Polk gazed suspiciously at him. "Okay, kid. We'll be in touch."

Snyder didn't put on the handcuffs for the ride back to town. They spoke to each other only once. "What are you getting out of this, Snyder?" Hooker asked.

"None of your fucking business," Snyder said. "And when it's all over, hunting season's gonna open again, Hooker. I'm gonna be making collections, and there's gonna be some interest due, too."

He stopped the car four blocks from the waterfront, and Hooker walked away without looking back.

Hooker knew he wasn't going to double-cross Gondorff. At least, he didn't think he was. The FBI man had maneuvered him into a corner. At the time, there was nothing he could do but agree. But he could get out of it. He could figure out something. Maybe he could tell them a phony time, that the sting was coming an hour or two after it really was. By that time Gondorff and everyone else would be on a train headed out of town.

Could he get away with it? Hooker walked toward the amusement park, wondering, glancing idly at the people he passed on the street. Polk said he would be kept under twenty-four-hour surveillance. And how about Gondorff? Was he being watched too? They seemed to know all about the play for Lorrimer. If they knew that, they also knew about the store. Jesus, what a mess. Maybe the only thing to do was tell Gondorff, and have everybody blow town.

The carrousel was running when Hooker arrived. Billie was in Gondorff's room, and they both looked up from a game of gin rummy.

"How's it going, kid?"

"Okay."

Billie was dressed for the night, her hair fixed, a tight satin dress over net stockings. She looked good. "Gin," she said. She dropped the cards and stood up. "Now you can play with Hooker. I gotta go."

Gondorff grunted sourly. "How in hell'd you get the ace of clubs? It was at the bottom of the deck?"

"How'd you know it was at the bottom?"

Gondorff gave her a look of disgust and turned to Hooker. "Sit down. Maybe I can win with an honest player."

Billie smiled and paused at the door. "Henry, things are a little slow tonight. Can I open the merry-go-round for the girls?"

Gondorff tossed her the keys and began shuffling the cards as Hooker sat down. "What's the matter, kid? You're not sayin' much tonight."

Hooker shrugged. "Just a little nervous, I guess."

Hooker fanned out the cards and rearranged them. He wondered if there was an FBI agent outside watching the building right now.

"Take it easy." Gondorff smiled. "You won't lose him now. I've seen enough to know."

Hooker nodded and played his cards indifferently. "How many guys you conned in your life, Henry?"

"Two or three hundred, I guess." He laughed. "Sometimes we played two a day when I was in Shea's mob. We had it down to a business. Like a production line." He picked up another of Hooker's discards. " 'Course, Chicago was a right town then. The fix was in. The dicks took their end without a beef. All the Wall Street boys wanted to invest our money for us. Even had marks looking *us* up, thinking they could beat the game." He dropped his cards. "Gin."

Hooker had nothing, a penalty count of fifty-seven.

Gondorff sat back and put his feet on the bed. "Yeah, kid, it really stunk. No sense in bein' a grifter if it's the same as bein' a citizen."

"You ever know anybody who got a fix with an FBI man? Bought him off?"

"The feds?" Gondorff laughed. "Don't even bother talkin' about it."

Hooker nodded. He slowly gathered the cards and smoothed them into a neat stack.

"Well," Gondorff said, looking around, "I'd better do some packing. I'm gonna be a hot number again after tomorrow."

"Then why you doin' it?"

The question was directed to himself as much as to Gondorff. There was a vague hope in Hooker's mind that maybe the old man might put things in some kind of perspective. But Gondorff only smiled.

"Seems worthwhile, doesn't it?"

"Yeah, I guess so," Hooker said. He got up slowly. He opened the door and then paused. "Henry?"

"Yeah."

"Listen, I appreciate your stickin' your neck out for me. I wouldn't have asked ya if it weren't for Luther."

Gondorff smiled gently at him. "Ain't nothin' gonna make up for Luther, kid. Revenge is for suckers. I been griftin' thirty years and never got any."

Hooker nodded, standing silently at the open door.

Gondorff chuckled. "Just get some sleep, kid. Think about sitting under a palm tree out in California for the rest of your life."

Hooker smiled weakly. "Yeah," he murmured, and left.

On the boardwalk only a few scattered booths were open. He couldn't go home. His four-fingered neighbor was probably waiting for him, planning to give him a fast-trip from the window to the street. And he had to think about tomorrow—how to complete the play on Lorrimer and beat the FBI at the same time.

Hooker walked south until midnight. Then, with the street lights dimming and the traffic thinned down to a few cars, he headed back north. He should have killed Lorrimer when he had the chance, on the train that night, or when he was riding in his car. When they were stopped at a signal, he could have shoved a knife in his gut and run from the car. What the hell was the difference? Lorrimer's men were trying to kill him anyway.

At two o'clock he arrived back at Angie's. The diner was empty. He stood across the street in the shadows watching Loretta give the counter a final wipe with her towel. She pulled on her coat, and turned out the lights one by one.

Hooker didn't know exactly why, but he followed her. He stayed half a block behind until she turned into an old building with a washed-out sign saying "ROOMS TO LET." From across the street he watched until a window lighted up on the second floor.

He wondered what the hell he was doing here. He hardly knew the girl. There were probably a hundred other men who came into the diner who knew her better than he did. And yet he felt a kinship with her. Tonight he too wanted to catch a train for somewhere. And it didn't matter where. He crossed the street and climbed the wooden stairs.

He paused at her door, feeling stupid. But he would feel just as stupid wandering the streets all night. He knocked lightly.

The shocked look on her face when she opened the door made him feel more foolish than ever. She was wearing a flannel robe, and there was a towel and a bottle of shampoo in her hand.

"Hi," Hooker said. He took a hand out of a pocket, rubbed his upper lip, and put it back. "I ... uh, thought you might like to go out and have a drink or something." He forced a smile.

She was speechless for a while. "You're movin' a little fast, aren't you?"

Jesus, Hooker thought, he felt like a kid asking for his first date. "Yeah, well, I don't mean nothin' by it." He shrugged. "I mean, I just don't know many regular girls."

She gave a short laugh, as if suddenly amused by this sorry performance. She shook her head. "So you figure I'm not a regular girl, and you expect me to tumble. Just like that."

"No." Hooker smiled. "If I expected something, I wouldn't still be standing out here in the hall."

She had to reconsider him now. Maybe he was on the level after all. He didn't seem drunk or ready to strong-arm her. She rested her free hand on the door frame, her stiffness easing a little. "I don't even know you," she said.

"You know me," he said quietly. "I'm just like you. It's two in the morning, and I don't know nobody."

She gazed silently at him for a long time. Then she nodded faintly, and gently pushed the door open.

VI. *The Sting*

Hooker awakened with a start. He was in strange surroundings—a bare light bulb dangling overhead, an old painted dresser, a table, and sun streaming in the window. He looked to his left, at the small bedstand and its urgently jangling telephone.

He was in Loretta's room. The rumpled bed beside him was empty, his clothes draped across the chair in the corner. Hooker dropped back on the pillow and looked over at the phone as it rang for the third time. Should he answer it? He ignored it through three more rings, wondering why Loretta spent money on a telephone. He'd never seen a phone in the room of a cheap boardinghouse. He reached over and brought it back to his chest, lifting the receiver. "Hullo?"

"Hello, Hooker," a bored voice said. It was Polk, the FBI man. "You really enjoy walking, don't ya? You tryin' to wear my boys out?"

"Whatd'ya want?" Hooker muttered.

"I figure you're going to make the sting today. What time, Hooker?"

"Three-thirty," Hooker said without hesitating. It was the only way he could figure to throw them off. They probably had the store under surveillance, but if Lorrimer came at one and they made the sting quickly, they might be able to get out before Polk had time to bring all his troops down.

"You sure?"

"Yeah," Hooker said. "There might be a little action earlier in the afternoon, but that'll be just for show. The big man comes at three-thirty."

"Okay," Polk said. "Who's your girl friend?"

Hooker felt his face flush. "I thought you guys knew everything."

"You just be careful, sonny," Polk said after a pause. "A guy named Cole got his head blown off last night. They found his body in a sewer about a block down the street from that rat trap you're in. You didn't happen to know him, did you?"

"Never heard of him."

"You know anybody named Salino?"

"No."

There was silence, then, "Okay, Hooker, we'll see you around three-thirty."

Hooker clapped the receiver into the hook and put the phone back on the table. He stared at the ceiling for another ten minutes, wondering about Loretta. They had made love twice before falling asleep. She had been responsive, apparently as hungry as he had been. And still she seemed to hold back, as if studying him from a distance and finding something amusing in his presence. When he questioned her about herself, she had answered with the same brusque cynicism she used in the diner. When it was over, she just turned away and went to sleep.

Hooker checked the top drawer of the dresser and found a safety razor. He shaved and cleaned up in the bathroom down the hall.

It wasn't going to work. Somehow, deep inside him, he had a feeling of doom, that the day was going to end in disaster. Lorrimer would not show up. Or Polk would have his whole crew watching the store and would bust in the minute Lorrimer showed. Or the four-fingered man would catch him along the way. He had tried to cut too many corners in the last couple of days, something Luther had always warned him about. But if they folded the con, he'd never get another chance at Lorrimer.

He pushed the thoughts from his mind and turned from the window, straightening the bed a little. He lifted Loretta's pillow to fluff it a little, then stopped. The note on the piece of paper said: "See you at the diner for breakfast."

At the Sherman Hotel, Amon Lorrimer had finished breakfast and pushed the tray to the side of the desk. He sat back, idly cleaning his fingernails while Al Coombs talked. Coombs had found out nothing about Shaw and his bookie operation. He had made inquiries with other gambling operators in town, and at City Hall. Nobody knew him.

"You think he's legit?" Coombs asked when he was through.

It was typical of Coombs, trying to cover his incompetence by suggesting that maybe Shaw and his whole operation were a figment of Lorrimer's imagination. Lorrimer had already decided to get someone else to run the Chicago operation. Shaw was probably grossing a million or two a month over there, and nobody even knew about it.

"I *know* it's legit," Lorrimer said irritably. "I've seen it. And that bastard is taking all the fat money out of this town while you guys suck your thumbs."

Coombs nodded uncomfortably. "You want us to move in on him?"

"Move in on him, shit," Lorrimer said. He tossed the nail file on the desk and stood up. "How the hell you gonna move in on somebody you can't even find? Never mind movin' in on him. I'm gonna take care of this myself. After today, Shaw ain't gonna exist anymore."

He never should have sent Coombs to Chicago in the first place. Coombs had been a good trigger man. That's what he should have stayed. A man needed some brains and imagination to keep an operation going and make it grow.

Lorrimer glanced over at the bodyguard near the door. "Lou? When did you say that plane was coming in?"

"Ten o'clock. The package oughta be here any minute."

Lorrimer nodded and moved back toward the desk. "Okay," he said to Coombs, "how about that grifter? What's happened?"

Coombs perked up a little, happy to report some good news for a change. "He's gonna be delivered to the cannery before noon. Salino called me this morning."

"Dead or alive?"

"Any way you want him."

Lorrimer nodded. "If he's alive, put him on ice until tonight. Then give him the chute." He sat down, "Who got Cole last night?"

"Salino."

Lorrimer smiled. "That'll teach you to hire pros."

There was a light knock, and the door came open. A heavy man with a fat briefcase came in. He moved directly across the room and placed the bag on the desk.

"Any trouble?" Lorrimer asked.

"No, it's all here."

Lorrimer stood up. "Okay, Al," he said to Coombs, "let me know when Salino shows up. By the way, I'll be catching the four-o'clock flight back to New York today. I want you to go with me for a couple of days. Tell Keyes to take over for you here."

Coombs blinked for a moment. He knew what the decision meant. He was finished as head of the Chicago office. He smiled weakly as he got up. "Yeah," he said. "Sure, Amon. I'll be there at four."

The man who had brought the briefcase sat down as Coombs left. "Leonard told me to tell ya two things, Amon," he said. "One, Moran's given us twenty-four hours to come up with the half-million. That's till midnight tonight. And two, a couple of the banks gave Leonard some heat about the checks. He says we gotta be sure and have that million back by ten in the morning."

Lorrimer looked at the bundles of cash in the briefcase. "Yeah, they'll get their fuckin' million back. And Moran'll get his pimp money." He smiled. "Lou," he said to the man by the door, "you better run out and get four or five more bags about this size."

The bacon was burned, and the hotcakes were cold, but Hooker was starving.

Loretta had been her cool cynical self again when Hooker arrived. She gave him a half-smile, handed him a grease-stained menu, and said, "You came, huh?" and went on about her business.

"How'd you like to leave town this afternoon?" he asked when she brought the hotcakes.

"Where to?"

"Florida, San Francisco, L.A., you name it."

"Suddenly you're a big spender, huh? How about a European cruise on the *Queen Mary?*"

"Sounds good to me."

She snorted and moved away.

Hooker smiled. He hadn't thought about it until he asked her. But it wasn't a bad idea. If everything went off okay, what the hell else would he have to do with the money? If it didn't, it didn't make much difference.

Hooker waited until she was alone by the cash register and took his check up.

"Listen," Loretta said before he could say anything, "could you do me a favor?"

"Sure."

"Angie wants me to go get some stuff for him, and it's kinda heavy. Could you give me a hand?"

"Yeah . . . well"—Hooker glanced at the clock at the back of the diner—"I'd be glad to, but I got some things I gotta do pretty quick. How about this afternoon?"

"No, he's gotta have it right now." She looked hopefully at him for a second, then shrugged. "Forget it," she said.

"I'm sorry, Loretta, but I really can't right now."

"Forget it," she said irritably, and turned away. She marched down the counter, scooping up dirty plates, banging them into the bin.

Hooker didn't move.

"Loretta?" he said when she stomped back to retrieve her towel, "how long you think it'll take?"

"About half an hour. But I wouldn't want to impose on your precious goddamned time."

"A half-hour? Why didn't you say so? I can spare half an hour."

"You sure?" she said, a trace of sarcasm still there.

"Yeah. C'mon, let's go."

She looked at him. Then she smiled. "Just a second while I tell Angie I'm going. Why don't you go grab us a cab?"

There was a cab parked half a block up the street, the driver standing outside reading a newspaper. Hooker whistled and held up a finger, and the driver jumped in. He pulled up to the corner just as Loretta came out with her purse.

"The Lakeview Cannery," she told him when they got in. "It's at the waterfront, just off Maxwell."

"Yes, ma'am."

As they pulled away, Hooker picked up Loretta's hand and gently squeezed it. There was no response.

"Look," Hooker said, "I was really serious about

going away. I'm leaving this afternoon. If you can't come along today, maybe I could send you the money."

She gave him the thin smile again. "Sounds interesting."

"Yeah. Well, think about it. Maybe I can call you before I go."

She nodded and looked out the window.

"Whatd'ya have to pick up at the cannery?"

"Fish," she said, and drew her hand away.

Hooker smiled. "That makes sense, I guess." She didn't feel like talking, so the smart thing to do was keep quiet. Maybe taking her along with him wasn't such a good idea, after all.

This was funny. In about two hours he was going to help touch a guy for a million in cold cash. And here he was riding out to a cannery to help a girl pick up five bucks' worth of fish. He wondered if the trip was even worth the cabfare. He looked over at the meter for a second and then frowned. The cabby had forgotten to hit the flag. The meter still registered zero. Hooker looked at it for a minute and then stared at the driver.

The man's cap was pulled low over his eyes. But there was something alarmingly familiar about the thick neck and jaw. Was it possible? He glanced at Loretta and edged a few inches forward, straightening to see over the seat. The man's right hand was resting on the bottom of the steering wheel. He was wearing a black glove, and the middle finger was missing.

"What's the matter?" Loretta asked.

Hooker eased back and took a long breath. Jesus, where the hell were his brains? Gondorff had told him Lorrimer owned a cannery. He looked quickly at Loretta.

"Who told you to go to the Lakeview Cannery?"

"Angie. Why?"

"Did he tell you to take a cab?"

"Yes."

Oh, shit, Hooker thought. And the cab was waiting a half-block up the street. They must have slipped Angie a hundred bucks to set him up. "Did Angie tell you to bring me along?"

Loretta looked surprised. "Well, yes, as a matter of fact, he did. Why? What's the matter?"

"Nothing," Hooker said. He looked out the side window. They were going about thirty-five. There were a few buildings on the left, empty fields on the right. The FBI, Hooker thought desperately. He looked out the back window. There was nothing, only a bus about half a mile back. Where was the great special agent Polk when he needed him?"

He glanced at the cabby's rear-view mirror, then fixed a smile on his face as he turned back to Loretta. "Listen," he said, "I'm in big trouble."

"What're you talking about?"

"Shut up and just listen. I'm going to stop this cab. And as soon as I do it, you get out that door and run as fast as you can. You understand?"

"No."

"Just do it. Believe me, it's important."

She frowned and picked up her purse, clutching it tightly in her lap.

Hooker waited another two minutes, his heart pounding, watching the road and the driver in front of him. The man's neck was stiff, his eyes glancing only occasionally at the mirror. Hooker edged quietly forward and braced his feet. There was no curb between the road and the empty fields on the right, and the man had only one hand resting lightly on the wheel. Hooker placed a hand on the back of the seat. *Now*, he told himself.

He lunged past the driver's shoulder. In the same movement he grasped the steering wheel and swung it abruptly to the right. Loretta let out a half-scream, as the car skidded off the road, bouncing and whirling wildly into the plowed field.

The turn threw both of them off balance. Hooker was sprawled across the driver, half in the front and half in the back seat. The car tilted and then jolted to a stop.

Hooker had his hand inside the man's coat. The man twisted away, at the same time pushing viciously at Hooker's face.

The next five seconds were a confused jumble in Hooker's mind. For an instant, as he yelled at Loretta to get out, he had the gun. In the grunting tangle of hands and arms, the roughly textured pistol butt was in his grip. And then it was gone. His hand was wrenched downward and twisted away. Hooker glimpsed a heavy fist coming from below him, and then the side of his head exploded.

The rest was even more confusing. His head full of fading skyrockets, Hooker was suddenly on his keees on the floor of the back seat, staring incredulously out at Loretta, who was standing in the field twenty feet from the car. She had pulled something from her purse, and in Hooker's hazy vision seemed to be aiming a pistol directly at *him*. But as quickly as the whole ridiculous picture registered, she was gone. There was a deafening explosion only inches from Hooker's ear. Loretta's head seemed to snap back. The gun left her hand. It was suspended for a moment in the air, and then both of them were motionless on the ground.

Hooker closed his eyes tightly and opened them again, uncertain for a moment if he was seeing correctly. The four-fingered man was striding toward Loretta now, scooping up the gun she had dropped. He shoved his own pistol back into its holster and knelt beside the lifeless body.

Hooker turned away. He looked at the closed door behind him, turned quickly, grasped the handle, and quickly pushed it open.

"Stay where you are, Hooker!"

Hooker ignored the command. He scrambled out the

far side of the car, and quickly moved crablike away from the taxi. Then he stopped cold.

The man had come barreling around the car, cutting off Hooker's escape. He stopped about twenty feet away, positioning himself between Hooker and the road, his legs spread, his gun ready.

"Goddamn it, Hooker," he said tightly, "you're really hot to get yourself killed, ain't ya?"

Hooker stared at him.

The man took a deep breath and shook his head in disgust. He shoved Loretta's pistol into a back pocket. "Now, get your ass back in the car. In the front seat."

A big diesel truck and trailer was roaring past on the road behind the man. The driver gawked at them for a second, then quickly looked away.

Hooker moved back toward the cab, and slid into the passenger side. The man circled the car, slamming the two back doors. He sighed wearily and slid behind the wheel. "Gondorff hired me to look after ya," he said. "But if I'da known you were so goddamned dumb, I woulda charged him twice as much."

He tossed Loretta's pistol into the back seat. "That dame was gonna kill ya, kid."

Hooker looked out at the dead body, still too bewildered to believe it. He stared at the open mouth and the mass of red that was seeping into her hair. Loretta intended to kill him?

"She coulda killed me last night in her room."

"Naw," the man said. He dropped the gear lever into low and drove slowly over the plowed furrows. "Too many people'd seen her around there. And she woulda had a problem gettin' rid of the body. That dame was a professional. Used to work for Dutch Schultz. Name's Loretta Salino."

Salino. That was the name Polk mentioned to him on the phone. Hooker tried to look back as the man pulled the cab onto the highway and headed back toward the city, but the car had raised too much dust for him to see anything.

"My contract with Gondorff was to deliver ya to the store, alive, by eleven-thirty today. So I borrowed a cab from a guy. I figured I'd be ready to hustle you down there." He laughed and shook his head. "Then you gets in with the dame, and I recognize it's Salino. She used to be a redhead. Then she says you wanta go to Lorrimer's cannery. I'm tellin' ya, that was really somethin'. Just about when ya made a grab for me, I was figurin' on runnin' outa gas. I was gonna park the car an' blow off a couple right in her face. Cleaner this way, though. We don't get no blood all over the cab."

Hooker nodded. He thought about his visit to Loretta's room last night and the note under the pillow, and the way she maneuvered him into going with her to the cannery. Jesus, and he thought *he* was a pretty good con artist. He was the prize mark of all time."

At a quarter after eleven Billie went to Gondorff's room to pick up his dirty dishes. Breakfast in bed had been her farewell treat for him. She knocked lightly and went in.

"Almost ready," Gondorff said from the bathroom.

Billie gathered the dishes on a tray, and Gondorff came out with a big smile. "How do I look?"

In addition to his tuxedo, he was sporting a new red cummerbund for the occasion. "Like a high-class con man," Billie said.

Gondorff bowed. "Thank you, madam."

"Watch your language." Billie sat down on the bed and watched him gather his keys and change from the dresser. "You sure you don't want me to work today?"

"No, we don't need you. Not unless you'd like to blow this town for a while. How about it? A nice winter in Miami Beach?"

"Hah! You'd better stay out of Florida the rest of your life."

"Okay. How about California? The land of milk and honey. Sit on the beach for a year or two and watch the waves come in?"

"Yeah." Billie scoffed. "In three weeks you'll get itchy feet and lose all that money to somebody else."

Gondorff laughed. "True. But we could have some fun, Billie."

"No, I think I'll just stick around here with the girls. I'm the domestic type."

She watched him slide a small pistol inside his cummerbund and then put three small rubber bladders containing reddish fluid into his pocket.

"You expectin' trouble?" she asked.

"You never know."

"Or are you *planning* some trouble?"

Gondorff smiled over his shoulder and straightened his tie in the mirror. "You never know," he said again.

He looked around the room. He had everything. He picked up his suitcase and gave Billie a friendly pat on the rear as she stood up.

"It's been fun, kid."

Billie smiled sadly. "You'll be back."

"Yeah. Sooner or later." He smiled at her again. Then he winked and walked away, around the carrousel and out toward the boardwalk.

Billie watched him, feeling a little lump in her throat. As he rounded the corner and disappeared, a door slammed on the balcony above her.

"Billie!" one of the girls screamed. She was leaning over the railing, her bare breasts dangling in the air. "Beatrice has my bra, and she won't give it back!"

Another door slammed, and Beatrice appeared wearing the bra. "I do not!" she screeched. "She just wore my bra all last week, and now she thinks it's hers!"

Billie sighed and headed for the stairs.

Special agent Polk, Lieutenant Snyder and the six federal agents ate their corned-beef sandwiches in silence. They had been sitting in the shipping office of the warehouse since Polk called Hooker at ten o'clock. Snyder had listened in on the call. Snyder suggested that he go back to work and meet them at Gondorff's store around three. But Polk had told him to stick around, he didn't want to risk any foul-ups.

Snyder had gone to the can a couple of times. His efforts to strike up conversations with the agents had brought him nothing but grunts, and he'd given it up.

At eleven o'clock one of the agents went out for sandwiches and coffee, and they ate them in silence.

"How about the press?" Snyder asked when he was finished. "We gonna tip 'em about the raid?"

"Nope," Polk said.

"It's good publicity for you guys. Good for your whole department."

"After it's over and we book 'em," Polk said, "you can pose for all the pictures you want down at the courthouse."

Snyder nodded, satisfied. It didn't make much difference where the pictures were taken, just so long as he got in them. Suddenly everyone around him was moving. It was as if Polk had given some kind of silent signal. The men were all putting their shoulder holsters on.

"What's goin' on?" Snyder asked.

"We're moving."

"You mean to Gondorff's? It's only eleven-thirty. Hooker said the sting wasn't till three-thirty."

Polk smiled. "You wouldn't take the word of a punk street grifter, would you, Snyder?"

"No, but ... I mean, why go so early?"

"Because I figure it'll come around one o'clock. The same as the first two times."

"Oh," Snyder said. He decided not to ask what Polk meant by the first two times. They seemed to have a pretty complete book on Gondorff's operation.

They drove off in four unmarked cars, Polk and Snyder in the lead. Polk pulled in behind a parked car, about half a block from Gondorff's. The others parked a block behind him.

"That drugstore on the corner," Polk said, pointing ahead, "is where the mark gets the phone call. Across the street in the corner room of that apartment house they have a lookout. He warns them when the mark is coming, so the whole show can go into action. The store itself is around the corner, about a hundred feet down that alley." Polk looked at him, and Snyder nodded. "Now," Polk went on, "after we see the mark go in, we'll give 'em four or five minutes. That'll be time enough for them to start calling the race. Then I'll give the signal, and we move in. McNeil will come around the back side of the alley, and we'll pull in up there. You understand that?"

"Yeah." Snyder nodded.

"Okay. Now, here's what I want you to do. Whoever they're playing for is bound to be a big wheel. Knowing how Gondorff operates, I'd guess he's shooting for half a million or more."

Snyder whistled softly.

"Okay," Polk said, "you've got the picture. Anybody who can come up with that kind of money has got to be important. So as soon as we're inside, I want you to get the mark out of there as fast as possible. You never know when a couple of smart-ass reporters are going to show up. And we can't afford to embarrass any big shots. You know what I mean."

Snyder smiled to himself. This could be a bigger boost for his career than he had thought.

Polk suddenly caught sight of something out the window. "There's your friend," he said.

Snyder leaned to the side to see past the car in front of them. A cab had pulled up next to the alley. Hooker and the driver got out and disappeared down the alley.

"Is the cabby part of it?"

Polk shook his head. "I don't know. We lost Hooker for a while this morning. I'm glad to see him back."

After four or five minutes the cabby came out and drove off.

Polk looked at his watch. "Okay," he said, "we've got about an hour to go. They'll all be showing up soon."

Snyder brought a fresh cigar from his pocket and slowly unwrapped it.

At twenty minutes to one Lorrimer was dressed and ready. He had three bodyguards with him, but he carried the briefcase himself.

They drove westward in silence, through the heavy downtown traffic, across the river, and into the shabby streets of the South Side. A block and a half from the drugstore, Lorrimer told the driver to pull over.

For several minutes the five men scanned the traffic and the parked cars and the few pedestrians who passed. There was nothing unusual. A garbage truck went by spilling more trash than it picked up. A panhandler approached the limousine, but quickly moved on when he got a good look at the occupants.

"Okay," Lorrimer said. The car eased out, rolled smoothly forward, and pulled into the curb across the street from the drugstore. The driver stayed in the car as the other three men crossed the street and went in.

The waitress didn't bother going to the table. She watched the three men slide into the booth next to the telephone and then discreetly retired to the kitchen.

The clock over the fountain said three minutes to one. Lorrimer checked it with his own watch, and then sat back, idly turning a sugar bowl in his fingers.

He hadn't decided yet what to do about Carver and his partner at the telegraph office. He'd told them he would split sixty-forty. If the horse he bet today was five or six to one, they'd expect about two million dollars as their cut. It was too much. They'd probably be happy with several hundred thousand. And it might be a good idea to make them sweat a little for that. Maybe he could give them a little cash and string 'em along through five or six more bets. That little fink Carver deserved it for turning rat on his boss.

The telephone rang. Lorrimer quickly rose from the booth and picked up the receiver.

"San Antonio Handicap. Pimlico." the voice said. "Place it on Syphon at ten to one." The phone clicked dead.

Lorrimer smiled. Ten to one. It was twice as good as he'd hoped for. He picked up the briefcase and headed for the door.

The other two men followed him briskly across the street, past the limousine and into the alley. "You guys wait out here," he told them as he knocked, Hooker quickly opened the door.

"You get it?" he asked under his breath.

Lorrimer gave him a quick nod and stepped inside. The place seemed a little noisier than before. Behind the counter a half-dozen phones were ringing. There were four or five men at the bar, and ten or fifteen more drinking at the tables, arguing over racing forms. It looked like Shaw was having a good day.

Lorrimer crossed the room and stood behind the only other bettor at the window. Niles pushed a betting slip across the counter. "There you are, Mr. Kelsey, a hundred and ten thousand on King's Image."

The man left, and Lorrimer lifted his briefcase to the counter and snapped it open. "One million on Syphon."

"A million dollars?" Niles gaped at the briefcase and back at Lorrimer.

"That's right. On the nose."

Niles smiled weakly. "Hold on a second, I'll get the boss."

Lorrimer smiled to himself as Niles hurried away and came back with a fat cheese himself.

"What's the problem?"

"He wants to bet a million dollars on Syphon, Mr. Shaw."

"A million? To win?" The fat man looked like he had been kicked by a mule. He was all business now, his face tightening, looking from the bag to Niles. "Jesus," he muttered, "we lose a bet like that, it could break us."

Lorrimer smiled. "That's right, Shaw. An' if ya win, it could make ya."

Gondorff ignored him. "What're the odds on Syphon?"

"Ten to one."

Gondorff shook his head. "Lorrimer, you're even dumber than I thought."

"An' you're more gutless than I thought. Ya gonna take it, or not?"

The loudspeaker above them rattled. "Last flash for the feature at Pimlico."

"Well?" Lorrimer said.

"Take it," he said suddenly to Niles. He glared across at Lorrimer. "And the count in this bag better be right, Lorrimer." He swung the bag off the counter and strode away with it.

"One million on Syphon to win," Niles said gravely. Lorrimer shoved the slip in his pocket and moved to an empty table.

The last-minute bettors were hurrying up to the window now. Lorrimer sat down and glanced over at Carver. The kid was staring anxiously at him. Lorrimer nodded, and sat back as the loudspeaker clicked on.

"Good afternoon, ladies and gentlemen. This is Arnold Rowe, your track caller for the feature San Antonio Handicap at Pimlico. For three-year-olds, nine horses going a mile and a sixteenth. The horses are in the gate, and . . . they're off!"

Lorrimer fished through his pockets and found a cigar. He snapped off the cellophane, sat back, and stuck it in his mouth. Outside in the limousine there were four more briefcases to carry out the winnings. He smiled, thinking about the look on Shaw's face when he had them brought in.

"Around the clubhouse turn," the announcer said, "it's King's Image by a nose, Syphon is second by one, Key to the Vault third by a half, followed by Mr. Moonlight, Red Ridge, Moneyman, and No Charge."

Lorrimer half-closed his eyes, listening to the call, and then glanced over as the chair next to him moved. It was the guy from the telegraph office, Carver's partner. Twist was bursting with excitement as he dropped into the chair.

"Sorry," he said, "but I just couldn't wait. Did everything go all right?"

Lorrimer motioned him to keep his voice down. "Take it easy. Everything's all right. We got Syphon at ten to one."

"Hey, that's great." The man glanced around, listened to the caller for a second, then smiled at Lorrimer. "'Course, we won't get that much for second. Probably only about four to one."

Lorrimer caught his breath for an instant. *Second?* What was the dumb bastard talking about? He yanked the cold cigar from his mouth. "What the hell d'ya mean, *second?*"

"Yeah. You bet him to place, didn't you?"

"*Place?* I bet him on the *nose!*"

Twist's mouth dropped open. His face was suddenly white, his lips moving wordlessly. "On the *nose?*" he choked. "I said *place!* I told you to *place* it on Syphon. Jesus Christ, he's gonna come in *second!*"

Lorrimer gaped at him, his heart suddenly clamoring against his chest. Place? Place it on Syphon? How could he have made such a stupid mistake? A flash of dizziness hit him.

"Into the backstretch," the loudspeaker said, "it's King's Image pulling away by two . . ."

Lorrimer half rose to his feet. He looked at the man

next to him, at the chalkboard, the shouting people, at the speaker on the wall, and then at the betting window. Jesus, he had to do something! He had to get his money back, change the bet! Somehow he had to bluff his way out of it. He moved toward the window, groping numbly into his pocket for the betting slip. He was dead. He would be wiped out. He found the slip. He had it in his hand, and held it out as he reached the counter.

"Hey!" he said. "What the hell's going on here? You gave me the wrong slip! You made it out wrong."

The man behind the cage was banging a rubber stamp on duplicate betting slips. "Sorry, sir. The betting is closed. All corrections must be made before the race."

"Down the backstretch," the announcer was saying, "it's King's Image now drawing out, followed by ..."

Behind Lorrimer the crowd was beginning to shout. "Don't you understand, for crissake!" he yelled at Niles. "I asked for *place!* I told you a million to place, goddamnit! I want my money back!"

Niles was paying no attention to him. Lorrimer looked desperately for Shaw. He was nowhere in sight. Then the building rage suddenly snapped inside him. His hands shot through the bars. He had Niles by the lapels, and he yanked him forward. "Don't you understand, you son-of-a-bitch? I want my money back! Gimme my money back!"

Lorrimer felt an arm suddenly clamp around his neck from behind. He let go of Niles and twisted in an effort to free himself. But then his feet went out from under him. He was yanked backward, and slammed to the floor.

For an instant he saw only blackness. People were screaming wildly. The track announcer's voice was blasting names over the noise, and Lorrimer saw Shaw's red cummerbund above him. He rolled quickly to his hands and knees and dropped his hand for his gun. But then he froze. Something was wrong.

The shouting had stopped suddenly. Except for the loudspeaker, the whole place had gone silent, and Shaw was backing away to the counter, gaping off toward the door.

There were eight of them. They were moving quickly into the room, grim-faced, their guns drawn, spreading through the crowd. By their trench coats and skimmers, they were obviously FBI men. Jesus, Lorrimer thought, it was a raid! That's all he needed now. He looked off behind the counter. Shaw had taken the briefcase somewhere back there.

"Just stay calm," Polk was saying. He had climbed on a chair near the door. Lorrimer edged back to the bar. What the hell was he gonna do? Agents were frisking people, moving some of them off in a corner. Shaw was still standing at the counter. The clerk behind him was holding his hands up, his face pure white.

"And they're coming down the stretch," the loudspeaker droned on.

"Somebody shut off that goddamned speaker," Polk shouted.

An agent hurried past Lorrimer and went into the back. The loudspeaker clicked off.

With the sudden silence Polk lifted his chin, searching for Hooker in the crowd. "Okay, kid," he yelled. He waved his gun toward the door. "You can go now."

Lorrimer looked, and then felt a surge of anger rise in him. Carver was squeezing through, moving toward the door. Carver! The little son-of-a-bitch was a stoolie! He had double-crossed Shaw, and now he had done the same thing to him. He'd set up the whole thing and then tipped the FBI.

There was dead silence in the place now. Even the FBI agents watched as Hooker shuffled, head down, toward the door. What the hell had they paid him, Lorrimer wondered bitterly. Whatever it was, he'd never spend it.

Fuck it, Lorrimer thought. He had other problems

right now. He looked toward the counter again, and then caught his breath. There was a gun in Shaw's hand. The fat man's face was contorted, his eyes blazing, and he was lifting the gun, pointing it at Carver. He was crazy to do it with feds all around. But the look on his face said he didn't give a damn. And then the explosion came.

There were screams from the waitresses. The agents were going for their guns again, and Carver went down. Shaw continued firing, the gun jumping wildly in his hand. Blood spurted from Carver's mouth. Then all hell broke loose, and Lorrimer hit the floor.

Everyone was screaming now, diving for cover, and Polk was pumping bullet after bullet into Shaw's chest.

Chairs and tables were crashing to the floor. Agents were grappling with customers. People were lunging for the door, shouting hysterically, paying no attention to the commands for them to stop.

Lorrimer looked over at Shaw. He was dead, sprawled on his back under the counter, his chest a mass of blood. Lorrimer pulled his gun from its holster. He quickly flung it across the floor under the bar.

He could get past Shaw now, under the counter and into the back. He started to crawl, but then a hand grabbed hard at his shoulder, and he looked up. Snyder was leaning over him, shouting above the noise.

"C'mon. We gotta get you outa here! Hurry up!"

Lorrimer hesitated, then came to his feet. He looked back toward the betting windows, but Snyder was hustling him away. Lorrimer tried to stop, looking back, twisting to get free. "How about my money?"

Snyder kept him moving. "We'll worry about that later!"

They were jostled and caught in the squeeze on the floor. And then they were outside.

Special agent Polk fired two more shots into the ceiling as Snyder and Lorrimer stumbled out the door. "Get 'em up against the wall!" he yelled. "McNeil, don't let that guy get away!"

Agent McNeil grabbed a man who was crawling toward the door. The situation finally seemed to be in hand. Polk got off his chair. At his feet, Hooker was lying face-down in a pool of sticky red. Gondorff was under the counter, one knee up, an arm thrown out, his white shirt now the same color as his cummerbund. They appeared to be the only casualties.

Polk looked over the room and then moved to the door. He pushed it open and leaned out, looking up the alley for half a minute. When he turned back, there was a faint smile on his face. He gazed silently over at the men against the wall, and the agents in front of them. For a full minute everyone in the room was completely silent, waiting. Then the buzzer sounded.

A sigh of relief came from the crowd. The FBI agents all smiled. They shoved their guns into their holsters, and the men at the wall relaxed. Everyone was suddenly animated again, laughing and talking, slapping each other on the back.

Hooker lifted his head slowly out of the gooey red. He pushed himself to a sitting position, removed the broken rubber bladder from his mouth, and spit out the last of the red liquid. "That stuff tastes terrible, Henry," he said.

Gondorff laughed. He was standing now, carefully removing his tux coat. "Nice con, Hickey," he yelled to the man who was playing the role of Polk. "For a minute there I thought you were the real thing."

Hickey dropped in a chair and stretched his legs. "No problem, Henry. Snyder went for it all the way." He laughed. "You shoulda seen the rag he lit under Lorrimer."

"Did you see Snyder's face when the shooting started?" Someone laughed. "I think he wet his pants."

"What happened to Lorrimer's goons?"

Hickey laughed again. "When we came screeching up and piled out of the cars, they took off like they had rockets up their asses."

The boosters were hurriedly changing their clothes now, still laughing. The ones who had piled out the door when the shooting started were filing back in. Whitey Lohman came in with a big grin. "Hey," he said, "who won the race? I had a hundred and ten thousand on King's Image."

"No chance, Whitey." Hickey chuckled. "All the money is being confiscated. I gotta take it downtown for evidence."

Whitey snorted and headed for the back room to get his clothes. "Same routine every time," he muttered. "The dicks always end up with the dough."

Gondorff had gotten out of his bloodstained shirt, and was buttoning up a fresh one. "Okay, you guys," he shouted, "let's take this place apart. Benny Garfield's picking it up in ten minutes. And you can get your splits from Eddie down at Boudreau's tonight."

Hooker was sitting in a chair across the room, still wiping the fake blood from his face. Gondorff walked over, stuffing his shirttail into his pants.

"Well, you beat him, kid."

Hooker glanced up. "Yeah."

Gondorff laughed. "You don't look too happy about it."

Hooker smiled sadly. "You were right, Henry. It's not enough." He shrugged, and the smile brightened a little. "But it's close."

"You want to wait around for your share?"

Hooker considered it. He checked the handkerchief to see if he was still getting red stuff from his face. "I don't know. Send it down to Boudreau. Maybe I'll pick it up tonight."

"Okay." Gondorff nodded. "I'm gonna be taking off as quick as we get this stuff outa here. So I'll see you around, huh?" He gave Hooker a pat on the shoulder and turned away.

"Yeah, see ya," Hooker said.

Hooker got up and headed for the back room. He took off his tie and got his suit jacket out of the closet and moved toward the door. He brushed his hand across his nose, giving the "office" to Twist and Eddie Niles and Singleton. He went out and headed south.

The wind had come up again. Old newspapers and dead leaves were skidding along the street, piling against abandoned buildings. Hooker shoved his hands in his pockets and glanced briefly at the sky as he walked. "We got him," he said softly.

At the corner he crossed the street and turned west. The words were for Luther. But Hooker had no feeling of triumph, no sense of satisfaction from being able to say them. He'd rather have things back like they were two weeks ago. But there was no point in thinking about that. Luther was gone. And the guy who did it was paid back. There was nothing more he could do. He tried to push it out of his mind, and he walked south and then west again.

At the Wood Street freight yards he stopped and leaned on the chain-link fence, looking in at the trains. If he picked up that money at Boudreau's, he would probably blow it before it got warm in his pocket. And then there was Lieutenant Snyder. If Snyder saw him on the streets, he'd probably shoot him on sight. Hooker smiled. That is, if he didn't have a heart attack first.

Hooker watched the railroad men moving along the boxcars, locking up and banding the loaded ones. A half-mile up the track, two engines were backing into place, preparing to hook up. He wondered where they were going.

The men were moving toward the front of the train, past the halfway point now. There was no one at the rear. Hooker looked in both directions along the fence. He scrambled up and maneuvered himself carefully over the barbed wire. When he hit the ground, he was running at full speed.

ABOUT THE AUTHOR

ROBERT WEVERKA was born in Los Angeles and educated at the University of Southern California, where he majored in Economics. His other novels (besides *The Sting*) include: *Search, Griff, The Widowed Master, Moonrock, One Minute To Eternity* and *I Love My Wife*. He and his family presently live in Idylwild, California, where Mr. Weverka is at work on a new novel.

FREE!
Bantam Book Catalog

It lists over a thousand money-saving bestsellers originally priced from $3.75 to $15.00 —bestsellers that are yours now for as little as 50¢ to $2.25!

The catalog gives you a great opportunity to build your own private library at huge savings!

So don't delay any longer—send for your catalog TODAY! It's absolutely FREE!

Just send us a post card with the information below or use this handy coupon:

BANTAM BOOKS, INC.
Dept. FC, 414 East Golf Road, Des Plaines, Ill. 60016

Mr./Mrs./Miss _____
(please print)
Address _____
City _____ State _____ Zip _____

Do you know someone who enjoys books? Just give us their names and addresses and we'll send them a FREE CATALOG too!

Mr./Mrs./Miss _____
Address _____
City _____ State _____ Zip _____

Mr./Mrs./Miss _____
Address _____
City _____ State _____ Zip _____

FC—3/73